THE MILLION DOLLAR BITCOIN

And How You Can Profit

AF808396

Anthony Hall
Dan Hollings
Daniel Hall

Copyright © 2026 by Daniel Hall

All rights reserved. No part of this publication may be reproduced, distributed, or transmitted in any form or by any means, including photocopying, recording, or other electronic or mechanical methods, without the prior written permission of the publisher, except in the case of brief quotations embodied in critical reviews and certain other noncommercial uses permitted by copyright law.

Published by Real Fast Publications

Publisher's Cataloging-in-Publication
(Provided by Cassidy Cataloguing Services, Inc.)

Names: Hall, Anthony (Anthony Michael), 1986- author. | Hollings, Daniel, author. | Hall, Daniel, 1965- author.

Title: The million dollar bitcoin : and how you can profit / Anthony Hall, Dan Hollings, Daniel Hall.

Description: First edition. | Celebration, Florida : Real Fast Publications, [2026] | Includes bibliographical references and index.

Identifiers: ISBN: 9780943941301 (paperback)

Subjects: LCSH: Bitcoin. | Cryptocurrencies. | Investments. | Finance, Personal. | Digital currency. | BISAC: BUSINESS & ECONOMICS / Investments & Securities / General. | BUSINESS & ECONOMICS / Personal Finance / Investing. | BUSINESS & ECONOMICS / Bitcoin & Cryptocurrencies.

Classification: LCC: HG1710.3 .H35 2026 | DDC: 332.4048--dc23

Disclaimer

This book is designed to provide information about Bitcoin and cryptocurrency investing. It is sold with the understanding that the publisher and authors are not engaged in rendering legal, accounting, securities trading, or other professional services. If legal advice or other expert assistance is required, the services of a competent professional should be sought.

The content of this book represents the views and opinions of the authors based on personal experience and research. All investment strategies and investments involve risk of loss. Nothing contained in this book should be construed as investment advice. Before making any investment decision, readers should conduct their own due diligence and consult with qualified financial advisors.

While the authors have made every effort to provide accurate information at the time of publication, cryptocurrency markets are highly volatile and subject to rapid change. The authors and publisher make no representations or warranties with respect to the accuracy or completeness of the contents of this work and specifically disclaim all warranties, including without limitation warranties of fitness for a particular purpose.

Past performance is not indicative of future results. The authors and publisher shall not be liable for any loss of profit or any other commercial damages, including but not limited to special, incidental, consequential, or other damages.

For business inquiries contact Daniel Hall - halldanielj@gmail.com

CONTENTS

FOREWORD

by Kiana Danial

In 2011, Bitcoin was $11 and I said no.

One of my earliest mentors, Nathaniel Hansen, suggested I should buy it. And I looked at him like he'd lost his mind. "No way. That sounds way too risky."

What's crazy is I didn't say "that's risky" because I had done thorough research on Bitcoin and concluded it's risky. I said it's risky simply because I didn't take the time to do the research and understand what Bitcoin is all about.

If I'd bought just $1,000 worth? That would be worth over $5 million today, even after the crashes.

That moment—that single "no"—cost me millions. But it also taught me one of the most valuable lessons of my investing career: your sense of "risk" changes the moment you choose to understand something. Don't label an asset as "risky" when the real risk is simply your lack of fundamental knowledge.

Wall Street has a habit of dismissing things it doesn't understand. When I invested in Nvidia and AMD back in 2015, finance bros literally laughed. "Why would you buy those?" they said. "They're not going anywhere."

Fast-forward and those "nerdy little stocks" ended up becoming some of the biggest winners in my entire portfolio.

Same story with Triple Compounding. When I first introduced it, people told me it was just a cute buzzword. Meanwhile, it quietly helped thousands of normal people take control of their financial lives—and *Triple Compounding For Dummies* became a bestseller because of it.

And when I finally—*finally*—started researching Bitcoin and cryptocurrency in 2016 because a company in the UK paid me to do it, I realized something that changed everything:

The stuff Wall Street dismisses? That's usually where the opportunity is.

Not always. But usually.

Because here's the thing about "alternative assets" that the establishment doesn't want you to know: they're only alternative until they're not. Forex used to be alternative. Then it became a multi-trillion-dollar daily market. Triple Compounding used to be a buzzword. It's now helping people achieve freedom. Cryptocurrency used to be a joke. Now BlackRock has a Bitcoin ETF. MicroStrategy holds billions. Even governments are getting in on the action. Texas recently added $10 million dollars in Bitcoin to the state treasury.

Bitcoin isn't a moonshot fantasy anymore. It's no longer the Wild West speculation it was in 2011 when I first dismissed it. It's steadily evolving into part of the global financial landscape. And the people who take the time to understand how it works, why it matters, and what's driving adoption may find themselves better positioned as this ecosystem continues to develop.

That's why when Daniel told me about *The Million Dollar Bitcoin* at a conference, I was instantly hooked.

Because this book isn't hype. It's not "get rich quick." It's a clear-eyed, research-backed case for how Bitcoin could reach $1 million per coin one day — and, more importantly, what factors readers may want to understand if they're evaluating Bitcoin's long-term potential.

You're going to read about institutional adoption. You're going to see the data on supply and demand dynamics. You're going to understand the fundamentals that make this not just possible, but probable.

Am I 100% certain Bitcoin will ever reach $1 million? No one can be. But I am certain of this: having real information, real research, and a clear understanding of the landscape puts you in a far better position to make decisions your future self will thank you for.

If you've ever been dismissed for investing unconventionally—or if you don't have a finance degree, a trust fund, or some Wall Street bro telling you what to do—this book is your roadmap.

Because the biggest financial regrets I have aren't from the risks I took. They're from the risks I *didn't* take because I let fear and lack of knowledge stop me.

I passed on Bitcoin at $11. I'm not making that same kind of mistake twice.

Should you?

Read this book. Study the institutional adoption data. Look at the supply dynamics. Understand the regulatory shift that's happening right now. Then decide for yourself whether Bitcoin at today's price is an opportunity or not.

Do your own research. Make the smartest decision you can for *your* financial future—not based on what the establishment thinks you should do, but based on what the data and the inevitable trajectory of this technology are telling you.

Because at the end of the day, personal finance is personal.

And financial freedom opens doors that nothing else can.

Freedom doesn't come from approval. It comes from understanding and action.

And you don't need anyone's permission to pursue it.

Kiana Danial
CEO, Invest Diva
Author, *Cryptocurrency Investing For Dummies*
and *Triple Compounding For Dummies*

ACKNOWLEDGMENTS

Thanks to my father Daniel Hall who was my biggest collaborator who shared the heavy lifting of writing, editing, rewriting and re-editing as well as debating all the ideas and applying his publishing and marketing expertise to the effort.

Thanks to Elaine Wilkes for her keen editorial insights and detailed feedback and her recommendations to make things as easy as possible for our readers to understand.

Also to Dan Hollings for being my first mentor in the world of crypto and for always having fun facts and figures that so informed this book.

Also, hi mom!

"Is The Million Dollar Bitcoin wishful thinking or reality? It just depends on when you read the book."

Dan Hollings

CHAPTER 1

BITCOIN IS FOR EVERYONE: FROM MAIN STREET TO WALL STREET

Bitcoin's Wild Ride

> *"Nothing else in the world...is so powerful as an idea whose time has come."*
>
> – Victor Hugo

Here's a question that'll make your head spin: How does something go from being called "rat poison squared" by Warren Buffett to having BlackRock—the world's largest asset manager—launching the most successful ETF in history around it?[1]

Welcome to the wild and wonderful world of Bitcoin...

In the history of money, investments, and creating massive wealth... nothing—and we mean NOTHING—has ever pulled off what Bitcoin has.

Let us paint you a picture...

You want to talk about real estate? Fine. Buy a house in Carbondale, Colorado (the top-performing market for over 20 years) and you'd make a 460% return.[2]

Gold bugs always brag about their shiny rocks. Buy gold 20 years ago at around $400... you'd be sitting pretty with a roughly 500% return today.[3]

And if you were REALLY smart and bought Monster Energy stock back in 1994? (Yeah, the energy drink company.) You'd be looking at a 200,000% return over 30 years.[4]

That's the BEST performing stock of the past three decades.

But get this...

If you bought Bitcoin when it was 30 cents in early 2011... And held it to the all-time high of over $100,000 in December 2024... You'd be looking at a return of over 33,000,000%.[5]

(Yeah. We had to triple-check that math too.)

Now here's what most people don't understand about these explosive returns...

They're not happening in a vacuum.

While Bitcoin was going parabolic, something else was happening behind the scenes that makes Bitcoin's rise not just impressive... but almost inevitable.

The Federal Reserve printed approximately $3.3 trillion in 2020 alone—that's one-fifth of ALL US dollars in circulation, created in a single year.[6]

The government provided about $4.6 trillion in COVID relief throughout the pandemic.[7]

Here's Economics 101: When you print more money, each dollar becomes worth less. It's basic supply and demand.

So while the financial experts were calling Bitcoin "digital tulips"... smart money was quietly realizing something huge:

When dollars lose value, EVERYTHING priced in dollars goes up.

Houses. Stocks. Gold. Art. Classic cars. Pokemon cards. (Seriously, look it up.)

But Bitcoin? Bitcoin is programmed to be the exact opposite of dollars.

There will only ever be 21 million Bitcoin. EVER.

No government can print more. No Federal Reserve can "stimulate" the supply. No politician can promise more Bitcoin to buy votes.

It's mathematical scarcity in a world of monetary abundance.

And that's exactly why we think this exciting ride is just getting started.

A Star is Born

Born from a nine-page document written by what many consider to be a genius named Satoshi Nakamoto...

This monetary revolution has bested all the naysayers who said it couldn't work:

Skeptics? Check. Governments? Double check. Financial "experts"? Triple check.

In just 15 years, a single Bitcoin went from worthless internet tokens to over $100,000.

Now imagine—just for a second—a future where one Bitcoin is worth $1,000,000.

Sounds far-fetched, right?

But here's the thing...

Every time any government fires up the money printer (and they WILL keep doing it)... Every time inflation eats away at your savings account... Every time the national debt hits another "impossible" milestone...

Bitcoin starts looking less like a speculative gamble and more like a life raft.

Despite YEARS of people screaming "Bitcoin is dead!" (seriously, there's a website that counts the hundreds of times they've expressed this)...

Despite China "banning" it every other Tuesday...

Despite financial talking heads on TV calling it a scam…

Bitcoin just keeps. Moving. Forward.

Why? Because math doesn't lie. And the math says: unlimited dollars + limited Bitcoin = higher Bitcoin prices.

Bitcoin changes lives

Real lives. Real people. Truth.

Let us tell you about Laleh Farzan...

Laleh was doing something pretty revolutionary for a woman in Herat, Afghanistan—she was a computer network manager. Getting PAID for her skills.

But here's the brutal reality: In Afghanistan, women getting paid can be dangerous. Husbands, fathers, brothers... they often just take that money.

Also? Women can't even hold bank accounts there.

And with sanctions? No PayPal. No online banking. Nothing.

But they DID have cell phones and the internet...the only things Bitcoin needs.

So Laleh's employer had a wild idea: "What if we pay you in Bitcoin?"

Laleh thought, "Why not?" and got paid 2.5 Bitcoin for her work.[8]

Then things got ugly. REALLY ugly.

Extremists in the community heard about Laleh and her computer work. The threats started. The harassment escalated.

When the attacks turned violent... Laleh knew it was time to run.

What followed was a year-long nightmare that no human should ever have to endure.

Laleh and her family fled the country.

On foot. By car. By boat. However they could move, they moved.

Thieves stole their jewelry. Their cash. Everything valuable they'd earned over the years.

At one point, their boat crashed crossing the Mediterranean. Their belongings at the bottom of that sea.

By 2017, Laleh and her family finally made it to safety in Germany.

They'd lost their home. Their belongings. Nearly everything.

But there was ONE thing that survived that hellish journey...

The seed phrase that gave Laleh access to her Bitcoin.

(A seed phrase is basically 12 or 24 words that unlock your Bitcoin wallet from anywhere in the world.)

All she had to do was type those words into the right app... and boom. Her Bitcoin was there.

She used some of it to restart their lives in Germany.

And here's the kicker: While Laleh was fleeing for her life, that 2.5 Bitcoin was quietly appreciating in value. Why? Because while Afghanistan's currency was collapsing and Germany was dealing with inflation... Bitcoin was doing what it does best.

Being scarce in a world of abundance.

Now here's where this story gets REALLY interesting...

In 2017—the SAME YEAR Laleh was using Bitcoin to rebuild her life—Larry Fink went on CNBC.

Larry Fink—considered by some to be the most powerful man in the world. The CEO of BlackRock—the largest asset management company on planet Earth, worth over $10 trillion in funds.

He called Bitcoin an "index of money laundering."[9]

But then... seven years later...

This same guy went BACK on CNBC and said Bitcoin is "no different than what gold represented for thousands of years. It is an asset class that protects you."[10]

Plot twist?

His company launched the FIRST Bitcoin ETF on the stock market. These ETFs are a way to buy and sell Bitcoin on the stock market. And it became the most successful ETF launch in HISTORY.[11]

(We can't make this stuff up.)

And Larry isn't the only one who's done a complete 180. The Bitcoin graveyard is FULL of these 'expert' predictions that flip-flopped:

Jamie Dimon (JPMorgan Chase CEO): "Bitcoin is a fraud... worse than tulip bulbs... If you're stupid enough to buy it, you'll pay the price for it one day." (September 2017)[12]

Plot twist: JPMorgan now owns Bitcoin ETF shares and launched their own digital currency.[13]

What made Jamie's bank start buying Bitcoin? What changed Larry's mind? Simple. They finally understood what we've been screaming from the rooftops:

When central banks print money like there's no tomorrow... When governments spend money they don't have... When the purchasing power of your paycheck keeps shrinking...

You need an escape hatch.

Bitcoin IS that escape hatch.

This is the REAL Bitcoin story

For people like Laleh... it's hope. It's freedom. It's financial sovereignty when everything else has been stripped away.

For others... it's a port in an increasingly crazy financial storm.

And for others still... It's the opportunity of a lifetime.

But for ALL of us... it's a hedge against monetary madness.

On Main Street. Wall Street. And everywhere in between.

The implications are massive. The adoption is accelerating. And the money printing? That's not stopping anytime soon.

This is why we believe the Million Dollar Bitcoin isn't just possible...

It's inevitable.

To make that case, the rest of this book breaks down into three parts:

Part 1 talks about the beginnings of Bitcoin. We're talking nuts and bolts here. How Bitcoin went from internet funny money to literally saving entire countries when their economies imploded.

We start with the very first real world Bitcoin transaction—because every empire starts with a single brick. Then we dive into why smart people think Bitcoin is the ultimate "store of value" (fancy talk for "place to park your money when everything else is on fire").

But wait... there's more.

We also break down Bitcoin as a payment network. Because surprise—it's not just digital gold sitting in a vault somewhere.

Then we show you something that's even more surprising: Bitcoin is already sneaking into places you'd NEVER expect. Nation-states are buying it. Real estate deals. Life insurance companies. Even stuffy underwriters are using it as "pristine collateral."

Part 2 is where things get REALLY interesting...

This is about the suits—the businesses and governments who said "Bitcoin is a scam" five minutes ago and are now quietly stacking it like their lives depend on it.

We're talking about Fortune 500 companies using Bitcoin as their savings account. Small-town mayors putting it on their balance sheets. And the entire financial world, slowly (but surely) warming to Bitcoin.

Part 3 is where the rubber meets the pavement...

After we've convinced you that Bitcoin isn't just some internet Monopoly money, we get to the good stuff: How do YOU actually potentially make money from this?

But we're not going to say it's all rainbows and Lambos. We're going through the risks too—the scary ones, the "oh snap" ones, and the ones that keep Bitcoin maximalists up at night.

By the time you finish this book, you'll know:

Exactly why Bitcoin isn't just 'digital gold'—and why that comparison actually sells it short

How to calculate your own potential Bitcoin position (without betting the farm)

The real reasons governments and corporations are quietly stacking Bitcoin

Every major risk Bitcoin faces (we're not sugar-coating anything)

Practical steps to get started—or to avoid Bitcoin entirely if it's not right for you

We're not here to sell you Bitcoin. We're here to give you the information you need to make your own informed decision about whether the Million Dollar Bitcoin is inevitable... or impossible.

Ready to dive down the rabbit hole?

Let's go...

"Bitcoin isn't magic—it's math with momentum."

Dan Hollings

CHAPTER 2

FROM CYPHERPUNK DREAMS TO DIGITAL GOLD

The First Transaction That Changed Everything

We promised you we'd start with the very first Bitcoin transaction. Because every empire starts with a single brick.

And this particular brick? It involved pizza.

Picture this: A hungry programmer in Florida decides to order pizza. Nothing unusual there, right?

Except this guy paid with something called "Bitcoin." And those two pizzas just became the most expensive meal in human history.

We're talking about a $1.1 billion pizza order.[1]

But to understand how we got to billion-dollar pizza, we need to meet the digital rebels who dreamed this whole thing into existence...

The Rebels Who Saw It Coming

Bitcoin didn't just appear out of nowhere. It came from a group of people who were basically the digital equivalent of revolutionaries.

They called themselves cypherpunks and their goal was to preserve privacy and human rights using technology.[2]

These weren't some basement-dwelling hackers. We're talking MIT professors, lawyers, former Intel scientists, and cryptography legends who saw the surveillance state coming before anyone else did.

David Chaum invented anonymous digital cash in the 1980s with his eCash system, which was implemented commercially from 1995 to 1998.[3]

Nick Szabo created Bit Gold in 1998, which was a direct precursor to Bitcoin.[4]

Eric Hughes, creator of the Cypherpunk Mailing List, stated in his 1993 manifesto: "Privacy is necessary for an open society in the electronic age."[5]

Their dream? A currency that NO government could control. No banks could shut down. No politician could manipulate.

But they were up against the U.S. government literally classifying encryption software as "munitions" under the International Traffic in Arms Regulations (ITAR), and it took a Supreme Court case (Bernstein v. United States) to challenge these restrictions.[6]

When Bitcoin launched, they knew something unique and revolutionary had just entered their world and the real work was just beginning but finally... their dream had come to life.

The Day Bitcoin Got Its Price

But instead of starting with a roar Bitcoin did not even whimper...

In fact, Bitcoin didn't even have a PRICE for over a year after it launched.

Think about that for a second.

This thing that's now worth over $116,000+ per coin... literally had NO assigned monetary value.[7]

It was just... there.

Floating around in cyberspace.

A computer science experiment that a Florida programmer named Laszlo Hanyecz was tinkering with.

See, Laszlo wasn't just any programmer. This guy was a PIONEER. He created the first Bitcoin software that worked on Mac computers. He figured out how to mine Bitcoin with graphics cards instead of regular processors.[8]

Basically, the trillion dollar Bitcoin industry as we know it today would not be the same without Laszlo's contribution.

But on May 22nd, 2010, he was hungry.

And he posted something on a Bitcoin forum that would go down in history:

"I'll pay 10,000 bitcoins for a couple of pizzas... like maybe 2 large ones so I have some left over for the next day. I like having left over pizza to nibble on later."[9]

(The man had his priorities straight.)

An 18-year-old kid from California named Jeremy Sturdivant actually took him up on it.

Jeremy ordered two Papa John's pizzas. Cost: $25.

Laszlo sent him 10,000 Bitcoin.

That created the first Bitcoin price: approximately $0.004 per coin.[10]

Do the math on what those 10,000 Bitcoin are worth today...

(Spoiler alert: It's over $1.1 billion as of August 2025.)

Jeremy spent those Bitcoin a few months later when they were worth "a couple hundred dollars" to pay for travel.[11]

Every May 22nd, the Bitcoin community celebrates "Bitcoin Pizza Day." There's even a commemorative plaque recognizing this historic transaction.[12]

And Laszlo? He's basically a folk hero now.

The guy who accidentally created the most expensive meal in human history.

But here's what's beautiful about this story...

Laszlo doesn't regret it. Know why?

Because without that transaction, Bitcoin might never have gotten its first real-world value.

Someone had to be first. Someone had to take the leap.

And that pizza? It changed everything.

From Experiment to Digital Gold

But Bitcoin's journey from pizza payment to digital gold wasn't going to happen overnight. It needed a real crisis to prove what it could do...

Cyprus. Financial meltdown. March 2013.

Banks shut down overnight. ATMs stopped working. People couldn't access their OWN money.

The government basically said: "Thanks for the deposit, but we're keeping a portion of it" through what became known as a "haircut" or "bail-in."[13]

While everyone else was standing in bank lines hoping to get their cash, some smart Cypriots quietly bought Bitcoin.

Why? Because Bitcoin doesn't care about bank holidays. It doesn't need permission from politicians. It works 24/7, 365 days a year.

During the Cyprus crisis, Bitcoin's price surged from approximately $47 to $88 in just days, representing an 87% increase as people sought alternatives to traditional banking.[14]

That's when the lightbulb went off for a lot of people:

"This isn't just internet funny money. This is a lifeboat."

This is when Bitcoin went from being a misunderstood asset, traded by people on the dark web and began its new journey of becoming Digital Gold.

The Ultimate Money Test

Look, we know this sounds technical, but stick with us here—this is where Bitcoin gets REALLY interesting...

Anyone can SAY their investment is "the next big thing." But how do you actually MEASURE what makes good money?

Turns out, there are six characteristics that separate real money from pretend money:

1. Non-consumability (it can't be used up)
2. Divisibility (you can break it into smaller pieces)
3. Fungibility (one unit equals another unit)
4. Portability (you can move it around)
5. Verifiability (you can prove it's real)
6. Scarcity (there's a limited supply)

Let's see how Bitcoin, gold, and regular dollars stack up...

Non-Consumability Think of it like this: the best money is like a referee in sports—totally useless for anything except the job it was made for.

Bitcoin? Perfect. You can't eat it, wear it, or build with it. Dollars? Same deal. Gold? Mostly good, but people do make jewelry and electronics with it.

Winner: Bitcoin and Dollars (tie)

Scarcity (This is where it gets spicy...) Bitcoin: Hard cap of 21 million. Forever. Coded into the system.[15] Gold: About 1-2% new supply each year from mining. Dollars: Remember that money printer we talked about in Chapter 1? Yeah...

Bitcoin wins this one by a landslide.

Portability (Think back to our Afghanistan story...) When people flee with their lives, they can't carry gold bars. They can't access frozen bank accounts.

But Bitcoin? You can memorize 12 words and access your wealth from anywhere on Earth.

Imagine trying to buy a coffee by chipping off a piece of your gold bar with a hammer vs. just typing a few numbers on your phone.

Winner: Bitcoin (by a landslide)

Divisibility Dollars: Can divide down to cents (0.01) Gold: Can be melted down, but good luck making exact change Bitcoin: Can be divided into 100 MILLION tiny pieces called "satoshis"

You can send someone $0.0000001 worth of Bitcoin if you want to.

Winner: Bitcoin

Fungibility (One unit = another unit) All three do okay here. But Bitcoin has an edge because every transaction is verified by thousands of computers around the world simultaneously—it's like having thousands of security guards all checking the same ID at once.

Counterfeiting is literally impossible.

Winner: Bitcoin

Verifiability (How do you know it's real?) Dollars: Watermarks, special inks, holograms... and people STILL make fakes. Gold: Complex testing, expensive equipment. Bitcoin: The blockchain verifies every transaction automatically.

Winner: Bitcoin (it's not even fair)

The Scorecard

Let's tally this up:

- Bitcoin: 5.5 out of 6
- Gold: 3 out of 6
- Fiat Currency: 2.5 out of 6

Bitcoin doesn't just compete with gold and fiat currency...

It absolutely demolishes them.

The Path to $857,142 Per Bitcoin

Gold reigns supreme as of this writing with a market cap estimated between $20-25 trillion. It remains one of the most valuable asset classes on the planet.[16]

Now here's where things get even more interesting...

If Bitcoin were to reach gold's estimated market cap of approximately $23 trillion, each Bitcoin would be worth approximately $1.1 million.[17]

The math is simple: 21 million Bitcoin ÷ $23 trillion = $1.1 million per coin.

As we write this, Bitcoin has a market cap of approximately $2.3 trillion.[18]

So we're not there yet... but here's the thing:

Gold has been a store of value for THOUSANDS of years.

Bitcoin has existed for 16 years and more and more people are adopting it every day.

What This Actually Means for YOU

This gets personal...

If you own 0.1 Bitcoin today, that's potentially $110,000.

If you own 1 Bitcoin, that's potentially $1.1 million.

But here's the kicker about that 21 million limit...

Only 21 million Bitcoin will EVER exist.

Do the math.

(And that's assuming none get lost, which spoiler alert: an estimated 4-5 million Bitcoin are already gone forever.)[19]

So we're really talking about maybe 16-17 million Bitcoin for 8 billion people.

That's approximately 0.002 Bitcoin per person on the planet.

The Writing on the Wall

Bitcoin isn't just competing to be Digital Gold...

It's positioning itself to absorb and improve upon everything the financial system does.

While gold had a 5,000-year head start, Bitcoin combines the best characteristics of both gold and digital money while eliminating their biggest weaknesses.

It's got the scarcity of gold without the storage problems. It's got the portability of digital money without the inflation risk. It's built for our digital world, but it learned from thousands of years of monetary history.

And we're just getting started.

Because Bitcoin isn't just storing value anymore...

It's about to start moving it. Fast. Cheap. And without asking anyone's permission.

But more on that next...

"Bitcoin doesn't wait. It rewards those who do."

Dan Hollings

CHAPTER 3

INFLATION VS. BITCOIN - THE UNSTOPPABLE FORCE MEETS THE IMMOVABLE OBJECT

A Message Hidden in Genesis

On January 3rd, 2009, when Satoshi Nakamoto created the very first Bitcoin block (called the Genesis block), they embedded a newspaper headline right into the code:

"The Times 03/Jan/2009 Chancellor on brink of second bailout for banks."[1]

Think about that for a second...

While governments were scrambling to bail out "too big to fail" banks with taxpayer money, some anonymous genius was building a system designed to make those bailouts... unnecessary.

Talk about perfect timing.

But here's where the story gets REALLY interesting...

The $10 Million Prediction

Seven days later, on January 10th, 2009, a computer scientist named Hal Finney made an observation that seemed absolutely bonkers at the time.

Bitcoin was literally worth NOTHING. You couldn't buy a piece of gum with it.

But Hal did some back-of-the-napkin math and said: "You know what? If Bitcoin becomes the dominant global payment system, each coin could be worth about $10 million."[2]

Now, who the heck was Hal Finney to make such a wild prediction?

Hal was a Bitcoin pioneer from Caltech with an electrical engineering degree. The guy was the lead developer on Pretty Good Privacy (PGP) encryption—the foundation of digital privacy that we still use today. He was a pioneer cryptographer and "cypherpunk" who built the first anonymous email remailer.

Oh, and one more thing...

He was the first person to run Bitcoin software after Satoshi. The very first Bitcoin transaction? 10 BTC sent from Satoshi to Hal on January 12, 2009.[3]

There are even many people who speculate that Hal was actually Satoshi.

So when Hal Finney made this prediction it was little more than a thought experiment, read by few at the time but over time it has only grown in stature.

His logic? Global household wealth was around $100-300 trillion back then. Divide that by 21 million Bitcoin and... boom. $10 million per coin.[4]

At the time, this was like Jules Verne writing about going to the moon 40 years before airplanes were even invented.

Pure science fiction.

Fast forward 15 years...

Global wealth has exploded to $471 trillion.[5] And Bitcoin? It's consistently valued over $100,000, with its market cap reaching $2.35 trillion as of August 2025.[6]

Hal's "crazy" prediction isn't looking so crazy anymore.

The Age Tax (And Why Your Generation Got Robbed)

If you're a young adult, we need you to sit down for this next part.

The data is absolutely brutal. Real wages for most Americans have barely budged in 40 years. According to the Pew Research Center, "today's real average wage (that is, the wage after accounting for inflation) has about the same purchasing power it did 40 years ago."[7]

The federal minimum wage, when adjusted for inflation, is over 40% lower in 2024 than it was in 1970.[8]

Your generation pays almost 100% more for homes. College costs have gone completely insane. And every time you turn around, something else costs more.

This isn't an accident.

It's not because you're buying too much avocado toast.

It's the inevitable result of money printing.

And here's the kicker...

It's just getting started.

The Money Printer Goes Brrr (And Why That Matters)

Here's the thing about fiat currencies like the dollar, euro, and yen...

They have one fatal flaw: Governments can print them whenever they want.

And boy, do they LOVE to print.

Need to stimulate the economy? Print money. Bank about to fail? Print money. Global pandemic? Print ALL the money.

Let me give you the jaw-dropping specifics that should terrify you:

M2 money supply is basically all the cash and near-cash floating around the economy—think your checking account, savings account, money market funds, basically everything you could spend tomorrow if you wanted to.

U.S. M2 money supply went from $15.3 trillion in February 2020 to $21.7 trillion by April 2022—a nearly 41% increase in just over two years.[9]

To put that in perspective... they created more money in two years than existed in the entire U.S. economy in the early 2000s.

The 26.9% year-over-year growth rate in February 2021 was the highest growth rate ever recorded.[10]

Every time they fire up those money printers, your savings become worth a little less. It's basic math: more dollars chasing the same stuff = higher prices.

Welcome to inflation.

When Inflation Goes Full Tilt

Most of the time, inflation creeps up slowly. The Federal Reserve "targets" 2% per year. (Which means your money loses half its value every 25 years, but who's counting?)

But sometimes? Sometimes inflation goes completely off the rails.

Germany, 1923: People were literally burning money to heat their homes because it was cheaper than buying firewood.

A loaf of bread cost 200 billion marks.

We're not making this up.

More recently? Argentina, Turkey, Lebanon... These countries are watching their currencies evaporate in real time.

The playbook is always the same: Print money, promise it'll be different this time, watch everything fall apart.

The Bitcoin Difference

Now here's where Bitcoin flips the script...

While every government on Earth is busy printing money like it's going out of style, Bitcoin just sits there. Unchanged. Unmoved.

21 million coins. That's it. Forever.

No Federal Reserve chairman can decide to "stimulate" the Bitcoin supply. No politician can promise more Bitcoin to buy votes. No emergency can magically create more Bitcoin.

It's the ultimate immovable object in a world of unstoppable money printing.

The Pressure Valve

Think of the global financial system like a pressure cooker.

Every time central banks print money, they're cranking up the heat and pressure.

Most of that pressure gets absorbed by asset prices—stocks, real estate, bonds.

But only IF you pick the right stocks. Only IF you make the right real estate deal. Bonds? They don't even keep up with real inflation for the most part.

Where else can the pressure go?

Bitcoin acts like a pressure valve. It's the one asset that can't be printed, can't be manipulated, and can't be shut down.

When the pressure gets too intense, it flows into Bitcoin.

That's why Bitcoin spikes during every crisis:

Cyprus 2013? Bitcoin spiked. COVID 2020? Bitcoin spiked. Banking crisis 2023? Bitcoin spiked again.

It's not a coincidence. It's physics.

The Correlation Game

Want to see something wild? Check out Bitcoin's correlation with money printing:

2020: As M2 Money Supply exploded 26.9%, Bitcoin went from $7,000 to $29,000 by year-end. 2021: Bitcoin hit its all-time high of $69,000 in

November as money printing continued at historic levels. 2022: As the Fed tightened (M2 growth actually went negative for the first time ever), Bitcoin crashed to $15,500. 2025: Bitcoin reached new highs above $124,000 as markets anticipate renewed monetary expansion.[11]

It's like Bitcoin has become the world's inflation thermometer.

When they loosen money (lower rates, more stimulus), Bitcoin's price rises. When they tighten money (raise rates, reduce spending), Bitcoin drops.

But here's the thing...

Every time they try to tighten, something breaks. Banks fail. Markets crash. People get angry and vote for politicians that will do what they can to stimulate the economy which means… they're right back to printing money.

It's a Catch-22.

The Disappearing Supply

But wait... there's more.

That 21 million Bitcoin limit? It's actually lower than that.

Satoshi Nakamoto mined about 1 million Bitcoin and never touched them. Gone. People have lost private keys over the years. Gone. Early mining bugs and mistakes. Gone.

Best estimates? We're probably looking at 16-17 million Bitcoin that will ever actually be available.

Which makes Bitcoin even MORE scarce than we thought.

The Math to $1 Million Is Simpler Than You Think

Here's where Hal Finney's prediction gets really interesting...

Bitcoin's current market cap: $2.35 trillion[12] Global household wealth: $471 trillion[13]

For Bitcoin to hit $1 million per coin, it needs a $21 trillion market cap.

That's just 4.5% of global wealth.

Not 50%. Not 20%. Less than 5%.

Bitcoin currently represents less than 1% of global wealth.

So we're not talking about Bitcoin taking over the world. We're talking about Bitcoin capturing what amounts to pocket change in the grand scheme of global wealth.

Think about that for a second...

If just 1 out of every 20 dollars parked somewhere decided Bitcoin was a better store of value than whatever it's currently in...

We're talking about $1 million Bitcoin.

And every time they print more money... every time inflation eats away at savings accounts and government bonds... that 4.5% looks more and more inevitable.

"But Inflation Is Normal!"

You'll hear economists say moderate inflation is healthy. That it encourages spending and investment.

Here's what they don't tell you: Inflation is a regressive tax that hits the poor and middle class hardest.

The wealthy? They own assets that inflate with the currency. Real estate, stocks, businesses.

Regular people? They hold cash. They have salaries that don't keep up. They get crushed.

The Setup

So here's what we have:

On one side: Governments around the world printing money like there's no tomorrow, driving inflation higher and making your savings worth less every year.

On the other side: Bitcoin, sitting there with its mathematically enforced scarcity, absorbing all that excess liquidity like a sponge.

The unstoppable force meets the immovable object.

And every time the money printers fire up... every time inflation rears its ugly head... every time people lose faith in traditional currencies...

Bitcoin looks a little more attractive. A little more necessary. A little more inevitable.

But here's the thing about Bitcoin that most people still don't understand...

It's not just digital gold sitting in a vault somewhere. It's a NETWORK. And networks have their own special way of creating value that has nothing to do with scarcity or inflation hedges.

In fact, the network effects of Bitcoin might be even more powerful than its monetary properties.

Let's talk about that next...

"Most people wait for proof. Bitcoin rewards those who act before the proof goes mainstream."

Dan Hollings

CHAPTER 4

THE NETWORK THAT BROKE EVERY RULE

So by now hopefully you understand why Bitcoin is digital kryptonite to inflation.

But that's just Act One of this story...

Most people are still trying to value Bitcoin like it's a stock or a bond or a piece of real estate.

They're stuck in the old playbook, demanding: "Where are the cash flows? Where's the CEO? Where's the quarterly earnings report?"

It's like trying to value the internet by counting how many phone booths it replaced.

They're missing the entire point.

Bitcoin isn't just an asset. It's a network. And networks play by completely different rules.

Let us show you what we mean...

The Asset That Broke The "Value" Textbook

Traditional assets are pretty straightforward to value:

Stocks? Look at earnings, revenue, growth prospects. Bonds? Calculate the interest payments and principal. Real estate? Check comparable sales and rental income. Gold? Supply and demand, plus a 5,000-year track record as humanity's backup plan when everything else goes down the drain.

Then Bitcoin shows up and befuddles the world of finance and exists outside of every finance textbook ever written.

No cash flows? No dividends? No CEO making terrible or great decisions? No company headquarters privy to governmental or social moors?

Every traditional valuation method just... doesn't work.

Which is why most Wall Street analysts spent years saying Bitcoin was worth zero.

They literally couldn't figure out how to put a number on it.

In fact, there have been LOTS of misses on Wall Street trying to value Bitcoin.

These are smart people with advanced degrees and with teams in the thousands with billions in research budgets.

But they were trying to analyze a flying machine with a horse-and-buggy manual.

(More on the airplane thing in a minute...)

But here's what they missed...

The Four Horsemen of the Bitcoin Apocalypse

Bitcoin isn't run by a board of directors in suits. Instead, this financial Wright Flyer is powered by four groups of people who each have skin in the game and often overlap each other:

The Hodlers (aka Users): That's you, me, your cousin who won't shut up about crypto, plus massive institutions like Tesla and entire countries like El Salvador. As of 2024, approximately 28% of American adults own cryptocurrency, representing about 65 million people in the U.S. alone.[1] Everyone who buys, holds, or uses Bitcoin. Think of them as the true believers who keep the faith.

The Blockchain Wizards (aka Developers): The coding ninjas who build on top of Bitcoin and propose improvements. These are the guys and gals who speak in mysterious computer languages and somehow make magic happen with 1s and 0s. They're like the architects constantly upgrading the house while everyone's still living in it.

The Digital Gold Rush (aka Miners): People running massive computers to secure the network and mint new Bitcoin. They're basically digital prospectors with really expensive equipment and gambling problems. Except instead of pickaxes, they use warehouse-sized computers that consume more electricity than small countries (Also Chapter 8 discusses why Bitcoin is actually great for renewable energy projects).

The Volunteer Accountants (aka Node Operators): The unsung heroes who verify every transaction and keep the network honest. They're like auditors who work 24/7 for free just because they believe in the system. There is no Bitcoin without them.

No single group controls Bitcoin. But together? They create something unprecedented.

Think about that for a second. When's the last time you saw four completely different groups of people cooperate on anything without a CEO cracking the whip?

Why Networks Are Magic (And Why Your Brain Will Hurt)

Here's where your brain might hurt a little...

Bitcoin is what economists call a "two-sided network."

You know how dating apps work? You need both people looking for dates AND people willing to go on dates. If you only have desperate guys and no women (looking at you Tinder), the app dies. If you only have women but no guys, also dead.

Same with Bitcoin. You need people who want to buy it and people willing to sell it.

But here's the kicker about networks...

They start slow. Like watching-paint-dry slow.

Remember when Facebook was just for college kids? When Instagram was just hipsters posting pictures of their coffee? Today they are giants.

Networks follow this pattern: slow start, then BOOM.

The Phone That Changed Everything

Let us give you the simplest example of network effects ever:

If you're the only person in the world with a phone, it's completely useless. You can't call anyone. It's just an expensive paperweight.

If two people have phones? Now you can have one conversation. Slightly useful.

But when 100 people have phones? Each person can potentially call 99 others. That's 4,950 possible conversations.

When 1,000 people have phones? That's 499,500 possible connections.

When 1 million people have phones? Nearly 500 billion possible connections.

The connections don't just add up. They multiply. Exponentially.

And Bitcoin? Current estimates suggest there are approximately 106 million Bitcoin owners globally as of 2024.[2] That sounds massive until you realize there are 8 billion people on Earth.

We're only at about 1.3% global adoption. One point three percent.

More than 98 out of every 100 people on the planet have never owned Bitcoin.

Let that sink in...

The Three Virtuous Cycles (Or How Bitcoin Feeds Itself)

As Bitcoin's network grows, it creates these beautiful feedback loops that make it even MORE valuable. It's like a financial flywheel that feeds on itself:

Cycle 1: The Cool Kids Table Effect People see Bitcoin going up → More people think "maybe I should get some" → More people buy → Price goes up → Even more people notice → Rinse and repeat.

It's exactly like the cool kids table in high school. The more cool kids sit there, the more other kids want to sit there too. Except instead of popularity, we're talking about money.

Cycle 2: The Developer Magnet Higher Bitcoin price → More valuable ecosystem → Attracts top talent → Better apps and services → Easier to use → More adoption → Higher price...

Remember when using email required a computer science degree? Now your grandma sends TikToks. Same thing's happening with Bitcoin.

More money attracts the best and brightest minds. And when smart people start building cool stuff, regular people start paying attention and using that cool stuff.

Cycle 3: The Security Spiral Higher Bitcoin price → More profitable to mine → More miners join → Network becomes more secure → People trust it more → Price goes up...

It's like a bank that gets stronger every time someone deposits money. The more valuable Bitcoin becomes, the harder it becomes to break.

The network literally becomes harder to attack as it becomes more valuable and decentralized.

"But How Do You Actually Price This Thing?"

We know what you're thinking...

"Okay smartie, Bitcoin is a network. Got it. But how do you put a price tag on a network?"

Great question. Two models have emerged that actually make sense. And before you ask, no, we're not just making these up...

Metcalfe's Law: The "It's Like Facebook but for Money" Model

This was originally created to value telephone networks back when phones were attached to walls. The idea?

"The value of a network is proportional to the square of its users."[3]

Translation: If you double the users, you don't double the value. You QUADRUPLE it.

The mathematical formula is $V = n(n-1)/2$, where V is the value of the network and n represents the number of users.[4]

Let's say you have a WhatsApp group with 10 friends. Now imagine a WhatsApp group with 100 friends. That's not just 10 times better—it's exponentially more valuable because of all the possible connections.

Applied to Bitcoin, research has shown that over 70% of variance in Bitcoin's value can be explained by applying Metcalfe's law to increases in Bitcoin network size.[5]

Stock-to-Flow: The "Digital Gold Rush" Model

This model treats Bitcoin like a commodity (which it legally is in many places).

With gold, when the price goes up, miners dig more gold. More supply hits the market, price stabilizes. Basic economics.

Bitcoin's different. The supply is programmed. Every four years, the amount of new Bitcoin created gets cut in half. It doesn't matter if the price is $1 or $1 million—the code doesn't care.

It's like having a gold mine that automatically produces less gold every four years, no matter what.

Created by an anonymous analyst known as "PlanB," the Stock-to-Flow model has broadly tracked Bitcoin's price movements for over a decade, though it has faced criticism for some predictions that didn't materialize.[6]

But here's the thing about models...

Both of these have flaws:

Metcalfe's Law assumes all users are equal. (They're not. Michael Saylor buying a billion dollars worth is slightly different from your college roommate buying $50.)

Stock-to-Flow ignores demand entirely. (Kinda important for determining price, don't you think?)

Neither accounts for regulation, competition, or the possibility that people just... stop caring about Bitcoin.

But here's the thing...

Even if these models are 90% wrong, they're still pointing in the same direction:

UP.

The Prediction Dilemma

Speaking of being wrong...

Traditional finance has a spectacular track record of underestimating network effects. We're talking "Blockbuster laughing at Netflix" levels of wrong.

Remember when JPMorgan's CEO Jamie Dimon called Bitcoin a "fraud" in September 2017?[7] The bank now offers Bitcoin services to clients.[8]

Or when Warren Buffett called it "probably rat poison squared" at Berkshire Hathaway's 2018 annual shareholder meeting?[9] Berkshire Hathaway still won't touch Bitcoin directly, but they do own shares in Nu Holdings, a crypto-friendly Brazilian bank.[10]

The pattern is always the same: dismiss the network, then scramble to catch up when the math becomes undeniable.

But here's what's changed: Major institutions aren't laughing anymore. They're hiring crypto teams, launching Bitcoin ETFs, and quietly accumulating positions.

Either the entire financial establishment has lost its mind, or they're finally starting to understand something about network effects that their spreadsheets couldn't capture.

Our money's on the latter...

The Wright Brothers Problem

You know the story of the Wright brothers, right?

December 17, 1903. Kitty Hawk, North Carolina. Twelve seconds of flight that changed everything.

But here's the thing nobody talks about...

The "experts" said it was impossible. The New York Times published an editorial on October 9, 1903, titled "Flying Machines Which Do Not Fly," declaring that it would require "one to ten million years" of mathematical and engineering work for humanity to develop a flying machine.[11]

This was published just 69 days before Orville and Wilbur proved them spectacularly wrong.

When scientists first saw their flying machine, many refused to believe it. It didn't fit into any existing transportation category.

Was it a carriage? It had wheels. A boat? It moved through the air like a boat through water. A bird? It had wings but was heavier than air.

Bitcoin is the financial Wright Flyer.

It has the characteristics of so many things including...

A currency (you can spend it) A commodity (you can store it) A stock (it has growth potential) A network (it connects people) A protocol (it runs on code) A movement (it has believers)

People keep trying to cram it into one box. "Is it digital gold or internet money?"

That's missing the point entirely.

Bitcoin's power comes from being ALL of these things at once.

It's the first asset in human history that can serve as money, property, AND infrastructure simultaneously and it's doing it as the first private property on the internet.

That's not a bug. That's the future.

And every new participant makes the network more valuable for everyone already in it.

The Network That's Eating the World

So while everyone's arguing about whether Bitcoin is "digital gold" or "internet money," the network just keeps growing.

More users. More developers. More infrastructure. More institutions.

More, more, more.

We're watching the birth of the world's first truly GLOBAL financial network that doesn't answer to any government, any bank, or any corporation.

And that global reach? That's where things get really interesting...

Think about it: Every other payment network is tied to a country. Visa/Mastercard works because the US dollar works. The Euro payment system works because the European Union works.

But Bitcoin? Bitcoin works everywhere there's internet. It doesn't care about borders, politics, or whether your government likes it.

That's not just convenient. That's revolutionary.

And we're still in the early stages. Remember—less than 2% of the world has adopted Bitcoin.

What happens when that number hits 10%? 20%? 50%?

The math gets pretty wild pretty fast...

But there's something even bigger brewing. Something that makes the network effects we've talked about look like a warm-up act.

Bitcoin isn't just growing as a network. It's starting to compete with entire monetary systems. And when that happens... well, that's when the real game begins.

Next up: We'll explore what happens when an unstoppable digital network meets the very stoppable traditional banking system. Spoiler alert: It's not going to be pretty for the banks...

"Many people have and will continue to make millions in Bitcoin. These aren't insiders, they're action takers"

Dan Hollings

CHAPTER 5

THE GREAT CORPORATE TREASURY AWAKENING

"The best time to plant a tree was 20 years ago. The second best time is now. The best time to buy Bitcoin was 2009. The second best time? Also now." — Ancient Chinese Proverb (Updated for the Digital Age)

So we've talked about how Bitcoin is eating the world through network effects. But here's where the plot thickens...

What happens when businesses—not just crypto bros—start figuring out that Bitcoin isn't just digital funny money?

What happens when CFOs armed with Excel spreadsheets and decades of financial experience start running the numbers?

Spoiler alert: The math is so compelling it's almost criminal NOT to own Bitcoin.

Let us show you what we mean...

The Screen Printing Shop That Cracked the Code

Bowling Green, Kentucky. Population: 76,000.

Not exactly Silicon Valley, right?

But it's home to one of the most ingenious Bitcoin adoption stories you've never heard of.

Meet Mike Coffey and his team at BlueCotton—a screen printing and embroidery shop. These aren't tech entrepreneurs or crypto evangelists. They print t-shirts for a living.[1]

During COVID, they wanted to reward their employees for sticking around during the chaos. So they gave away $30,000 as bonuses.

Nice gesture. Everyone appreciated it.

Fast forward two years. They want to do something similar again.

Mike goes to their finance person: "How much did we give away last time?"

"I don't know; don't remember"

Mike was shocked.

"It was the most money we'd ever given away and nobody remembers it?!"

Now thankfully Mike had developed a personal interest in Bitcoin by this point and although he was taken aback by what he just heard, when he had some time to think about what to do, that's when Bitcoin came to mind...[2]

Mike had been watching his own Bitcoin investment grow, which sparked an idea: Instead of giving cash that disappears, what if he could give his employees a piece of the future?

And here was the big idea.

First, they bought $120,000 worth of Bitcoin mining equipment and then they made their employees an offer.[3]

If they stay for 5 years, they get their share of the Bitcoin earned during that time.

100% free.

For anyone who understands Bitcoin—that's a great deal..

For anyone who didn't understand (most of their staff) they set up the miners right in the warehouse where everyone could see them humming away. They put up a screen showing how much Bitcoin was being mined and how much each employee would get and the current value of their Bitcoin.[4]

Logan Thomason, a screen printer at BlueCotton, explained it perfectly: "The company views this as an opportunity to teach and educate us about long-term investing and digital assets. We get to learn about and be part of the Bitcoin network, which is both fascinating and promising. It's an excellent incentive for employees to join us and stay for the long run."[5]

Most of their employees had no clue what Bitcoin actually was. But they knew those machines were working 24/7, earning them something valuable. The screen updates every 15 minutes, so everyone can watch their nest egg grow in real time.

Mike Coffey, the CEO, put it simply: "Bitcoin was a perfect solution because it's truly scarce and decentralized, and it gives our employees a fighting chance against inflation."[6]

The results?

Their employee turnover dropped significantly.[7]

Do you know what employee turnover costs a business? It's not just replacing people—it's training, lost productivity, institutional knowledge walking out the door, and more. Mike and his team didn't just give their employees Bitcoin. They accidentally discovered the Holy Grail of human resources.

Since June 2022, they've mined nearly 4 Bitcoin. By 2029, they expect to have 6-9 coins total.[8] At today's prices, that's potentially over $600,000 to split among their team.

And this is just a tiny screen printing shop in Kentucky...

The Corporate FOMO Epidemic

But BlueCotton's genius move is spreading like wildfire through corporate America.

What started as a trickle has become a flood. Companies are getting serious FOMO watching their competitors stack Bitcoin while they sit on melting ice cubes of cash.

The secret sauce? Smart executives are finally doing the math that's been staring them in the face for years.

Let me show you exactly what we mean...

The Corporate Treasury Awakening

But here's where the numbers tell the real story. Zoom out and look at what's happening in corporate boardrooms across America.

River Financial ran the numbers on corporate treasury performance from 2020 to 2024. The results will make you question everything about traditional "safe" investments:

Companies that held cash reserves: significant losses due to inflation Companies that used money market accounts: better, but still losing value Companies that put just 3% in Bitcoin: positive returns[9]

Read that again.

By allocating just 3% of their treasury to Bitcoin—and keeping 97% in "safe" assets—companies turned a guaranteed loss into a solid win.

For doing basically nothing.

Want a real-world example of what the old way gets you? Let's talk Apple.

Apple sits on about $65 billion in cash as of 2024.[10] That's more than the GDP of many countries.

Over the past decade, they've been good little corporate citizens. Buying treasury bonds. Playing it safe. Following all the textbook rules.

Result? After accounting for inflation, they've lost significant value on their cash holdings.[11]

That's not a rounding error. That's real money just... poof gone.

All because they followed the "safe" playbook.

The Three Catalysts That Changed Everything

So why haven't more businesses jumped on this obvious opportunity?

According to industry analysis, three things changed in 2024 that made Bitcoin adoption dramatically easier:

1. The Regulatory Fog Lifted

For years, companies wanted to buy Bitcoin but couldn't figure out how to properly account for it.

The rules were murky. The lawyers were nervous. The accountants were losing sleep.

Then the Bitcoin ETFs got approved. Suddenly, buying Bitcoin became as easy as buying any other asset. The regulatory pathway was clear.

The numbers tell the story: 2020: Corporations owned 0.56% of all Bitcoin Late 2024: That number jumped to 3.3%[12]

That's a 587% increase in corporate adoption. In four years.

2. Fair Value Accounting (Finally!)

In December 2023, the Financial Accounting Standards Board (FASB) issued an update allowing companies to recognize Bitcoin holdings at fair value, effective from December 2024.[13]

Before this, companies had to use accounting rules where if Bitcoin went down, they had to mark it at the lowest price. But if it went back up? Too bad. It stayed at the lowest price on their books.

It was like being forced to value your house based on the worst day in the real estate market. Forever.

That rule change opened the floodgates.

3. The Global Money Printer Reality Check

Companies are finally waking up to the fact that they're not just competing locally anymore. They're exposed to monetary chaos from around the world.

When Argentina's currency implodes, when Turkey's central bank goes crazy, when any government anywhere decides to print money like there's no tomorrow—it can affect everyone.

Smart companies are starting to hedge against this.

And Bitcoin is one of the few assets that doesn't answer to any government.

The Underground Bitcoin Revolution

While everyone's watching the headlines about Tesla and MicroStrategy, there's a whole underground movement of companies quietly accumulating Bitcoin.

Over 145 companies worldwide are now holding Bitcoin in their treasuries.[14] Many of them are flying completely under the radar.

Here are some you've probably never heard of:

Metaplanet - A Japanese hotel company that's now Asia's largest public Bitcoin holder with 7,800 BTC (approximately $806 million as of May 2025). Their CEO wants to reach 10,000 Bitcoin by the end of 2025.[15]

The Blockchain Group - Europe's first Bitcoin treasury company, aiming to acquire 170,000-260,000 Bitcoin (approximately 1% of total supply) by 2033. Currently holds 620 BTC worth approximately $69 million.[16]

Even **Rumble** (the YouTube alternative) announced they're adding up to $20 million in Bitcoin to strengthen ties with their "decentralization-minded users."[17]

Here's the kicker: Most of these moves happened very recently. The momentum is accelerating.

And it's not just small companies. **GameStop** approved Bitcoin as a treasury asset in March 2025.[18] Marathon Digital raised $850 million specifically to buy more Bitcoin. Hut 8 launched a $250 million Bitcoin buying program.

Market observers are calling it corporate FOMO—the fear that companies are now scrambling to add Bitcoin before they get left behind entirely.

The MicroStrategy Moonshot

But if you want to see what happens when a company goes ALL IN on Bitcoin, you need to understand the MicroStrategy story.

Michael Saylor was running a software company that was... struggling. Stock price going nowhere. Business model getting disrupted. Standard corporate death spiral.

Then COVID hit.

Saylor spent his lockdown time studying Bitcoin extensively. Week after week of research into money, inflation, and this digital asset.

One day, Bitcoin was trading around $10,000.

Saylor made his move: $100 million. Just like that.

But Saylor didn't stop there. He turned MicroStrategy into a Bitcoin accumulation machine. Using debt, convertible bonds, every financial engineering trick in the book to buy more Bitcoin.

The strategy? Simple. Buy Bitcoin. Hold forever. Use it as your treasury asset.

The results? MicroStrategy's stock has performed extraordinarily well since they started their Bitcoin strategy.

As of August 2025, they now own over 628,000 Bitcoin.[19] That's more than 2% of the entire supply.

Saylor's goal? Turn MicroStrategy into the world's first Bitcoin bank.

The 207 Billion Dollar Question

Here's where the math gets wild...

According to Harvard Business Review, U.S. corporations are sitting on $6.9 trillion in cash reserves.[20]

Remember our earlier math? Just 3% in Bitcoin turns a guaranteed loss into a solid win.

3% of $6.9 trillion is $207 billion.

At just $100,000 per Bitcoin, that would buy 2.1 million Bitcoin.

And that's just American companies. We haven't even talked about European businesses, Asian conglomerates, or the thousands of companies around the world sitting on cash that's slowly being destroyed by inflation.

Think about this competitive angle: When Company A holds 3% Bitcoin and Company B holds 0%, what happens during the next inflation spike?

Company A's treasury grows. Company B's shrinks.

Multiply that across thousands of decisions, and Company A starts pulling ahead in ways that compound over time. Better financial flexibility. Ability to invest in growth. Ability to weather storms.

Company B? They're explaining to shareholders why they're losing money on "safe" investments while their competitors are printing gains.

So eventually, companies can be either on the train, or on the tracks.

The Inevitable Cascade

Think about what happens when this dam finally breaks...

Picture this: JP Morgan announces a Bitcoin treasury strategy tomorrow. Their stock jumps 15%. Every other bank CEO immediately gets phone calls from their board.

The second major bank does it. Then the third. Suddenly it's not news anymore—it's standard practice.

The companies that don't adapt? They'll be the cautionary tales—proof that sometimes the biggest risk is refusing to take any risk at all

We've seen this movie before. Remember when companies resisted having websites waiting to see if "this Internet thing" pans out? When they thought email was a fad? When they insisted nobody would ever shop online?

Here's the pattern:

1. Dismiss the new technology as "risky" or "speculative"
2. Watch early adopters succeed
3. Watch competitors adopt it successfully
4. Scramble to catch up
5. Wish you'd moved sooner

Except this time, there's a limited supply. Only 21 million Bitcoin will ever exist. And every day, there are fewer available.

The early movers get the best prices. The laggards get whatever's left.

What This Means for YOU

Whether you work for a company or own one, this corporate awakening creates opportunities:

If you're an employee: Start the conversation. Send your CFO articles about corporate Bitcoin adoption. Ask questions during company meetings about treasury diversification. The companies that get this right early will be the ones thriving in five years.

If you're a business owner: This is your chance to get ahead of the curve. Even a small allocation could give you a significant competitive advantage as inflation continues to erode cash holdings.

If you're an investor: The companies that adopt Bitcoin early and intelligently will likely outperform those that don't. It's another layer of due diligence to consider.

The smart money is already moving. The question is: How long before it becomes obvious to everyone else?

Beyond the Balance Sheet

But this isn't just about corporate treasuries making more money (though that's nice).

This is about a fundamental shift in how businesses think about money itself.

For the first time in history, companies can hold an asset that:

- Can't be printed by any government
- Can't be seized by any bank
- Can't be inflated away by any politician
- Gains value as more people adopt it

It's like having a treasury asset that gets stronger every time someone else decides to use it.

No wonder corporate America is having its 'holy sh*t' moment.

The Tipping Point

We're at that moment where the early adopters have proven the concept, but the mainstream hasn't fully caught on yet.

BlueCotton figured it out with their employees. Apple could have saved significant money if they'd allocated just 3% to Bitcoin. MicroStrategy turned a struggling software company into a Bitcoin empire.

The math works. The technology works. The regulatory clarity is there.

The only question left is: How fast will businesses figure this out?

Because once they do, the race isn't just about who adopts Bitcoin first.

It's about who can get the most before everyone else realizes what's happening.

And when that realization hits the corner office executives of the world's largest corporations...

Well, that's when the plot takes a wild turn.

But corporate adoption is just one piece of the puzzle. There's an even bigger player entering the game. One that makes corporate treasuries look like pocket change.

"When Bitcoin hits $1M, the question won't be 'why'
—it'll be 'where were you?'"

Dan Hollings

CHAPTER 6

I PLEDGE ALLEGIANCE TO BITCOIN

"People use Bitcoin as a speculative asset. It's like gold—it's just virtual and digital. It's not a competitor for the dollar, it's really a competitor for gold."

— U.S. Federal Reserve Chair Jerome Powell

So far we've watched Bitcoin seduce individuals, conquer corporations, and turn treasury departments into believers.

But what happens when entire countries start playing this game?

Spoiler alert: The biggest poker game in human history isn't about to begin. It's already started. And the stakes? Nothing less than the future of money itself.

Game On: The 2025 Reality

Picture the world's most exclusive poker room, except this time the game is real and the players are holding nuclear weapons along with their cards.

Around the table sit world leaders, and unlike our corporate executives from Chapter 5, these players control entire economies. Some have already gone all-in. Others are frantically calculating their odds.

Those orange chips everyone's eyeing? Bitcoin. All 21 million of them.

Here's what's actually happening while you're reading this...

America's All-In Moment

March 6, 2025: President Trump doesn't just talk about Bitcoin. He signs executive orders establishing the Strategic Bitcoin Reserve. Not a proposal. Not a study.[1]

The scorecard is revealing:

- Strategic Bitcoin Reserve: ✓ Established
- U.S. government Bitcoin holdings: ✓ Over 200,000 BTC (~$17 billion)[2]
- Trump Media Bitcoin investment: ✓ (Actual amounts TBD)
- Digital Asset Stockpile: ✓ Established for other cryptocurrencies[3]
- Multiple U.S. states with Bitcoin legislation: ✓ In progress

This isn't a government "considering" Bitcoin anymore. This is a government that looked at the global financial chessboard and decided to play three dimensional chess.

The message to every other country? Catch up or get left behind.

And catch up they're desperately trying to do...

The Global Response (It's Happening Fast)

The moment America made its move, finance ministers around the world started getting very uncomfortable phone calls from their presidents.

The Czech Republic jumped first. January 2025: Czech National Bank Governor Aleš Michl announced consideration of investing up to 5% of the country's €140 billion ($146 billion) reserves in Bitcoin. That's potentially $7.3 billion hitting the market.[4]

But the real panic is coming from the major powers who realize they're about to be left behind...

Germany's former Finance Minister Christian Lindner is literally begging the European Central Bank to follow Trump's lead. In parliamentary addresses, Lindner has called out European leadership:

"The new Trump administration is pursuing an extremely progressive policy when it comes to crypto assets such as Bitcoin... Germany and Europe must not allow themselves to fall behind again."[5]

The guy had four years as Finance Minister to make this happen, and now he's publicly pleading because he sees the writing on the wall.

Meanwhile, Brazil's Congressman Eros Biondini has introduced bill PL 2471/2024 to create RESBit (Bitcoin Sovereign Strategic Reserve), proposing to allocate up to 5% of Brazil's national reserves to Bitcoin. With Brazil being Latin America's largest economy at $2.6 trillion GDP, this could represent one of the world's largest national Bitcoin reserve initiatives if passed.[6]

Japan's got not one but two champions pushing Bitcoin adoption. Opposition leader Yuichiro Tamaki of the Democratic Party for the People has been grilling the Prime Minister about crypto tax reforms, while lawmaker Satoshi Hamada (yes, his actual name is Satoshi) is pushing for a national Bitcoin reserve, asking *"Should Japan also introduce a system to convert part of its foreign exchange reserves into crypto assets such as Bitcoin?"*[7]

Even Switzerland—the country that practically invented neutral banking—has constitutional initiatives underway to require their National Bank to hold Bitcoin alongside gold.

This isn't some distant future scenario. This is real change at the nation-state level.

But while the big countries scramble, something beautiful has already happened...

David vs. Goliath (Except David's Already Won)

While the superpowers circle each other like heavyweight boxers, the little guys have been throwing haymakers and landing them.

El Salvador made Bitcoin legal tender back in 2021 when everyone thought they were crazy. Though the country ended Bitcoin's legal tender status in January 2025 under pressure from the IMF for a $1.4 billion loan, they still maintain over 6,000 Bitcoin in reserves worth approximately $635 million.[8] That strategic accumulation during the early years may prove prescient.

Bhutan—a country most people can't find on a map—quietly revealed they're among the world's largest nation-state Bitcoin holders. They've been mining Bitcoin in the Himalayas while everyone else was debating whether crypto was "real money."

These weren't Hail Mary passes. These were calculated bets on the future of money, made when the odds were still good.

Now here's the math that's keeping finance ministers awake at night...

The Supply Math That Breaks Everything

Here's the number that's keeping every finance minister awake at night: 21 million.

That's it. That's all the Bitcoin that will ever exist.

Now consider this:

- 195 countries in the world
- Most want some Bitcoin for their reserves
- Universities, pension funds, and sovereign wealth funds also want in
- Oh, and individuals and corporations aren't stopping their buying

If every country wanted just 50,000 Bitcoin for their reserves (a modest amount), we'd need 9.75 million coins. That's nearly half the total supply. Just for governments.

Also, consider governmental sub-units. New Hampshire became the first U.S. state to establish a Bitcoin reserve (up to 5% of state funds) in May

2025.[9] Arizona and other states are following. Wisconsin's pension fund bought over $160 million in Bitcoin ETFs.[10]

The math is simple: There isn't enough Bitcoin for everyone who wants it.

And when governments join the network, something incredible happens...

When Governments Create Network Effects

Remember how we talked about network effects making Bitcoin more valuable as more people use it?

Well, when governments start joining that network, the effect doesn't just accelerate—it goes supernova.

Here's why: Every country that adds Bitcoin to their reserves sends a signal to every other country that Bitcoin is legitimate money. Every trade deal settled in Bitcoin creates real-world demand. Every sanction bypassed with Bitcoin proves its utility as neutral money.

But it's not just governments anymore. Harvard invested $117 million into Bitcoin ETFs. State pension funds are buying Bitcoin ETFs. The entire institutional infrastructure of society is quietly rotating into Bitcoin.

When your state pension fund holds Bitcoin, when your university endowment is buying it, when your government treats it as a strategic asset... Bitcoin stops being an "alternative" investment and starts being just an "investment."

We're approaching the point where this becomes unstoppable...

The Point of No Return

We're fast approaching what economists call a "Nash Equilibrium"—the point where no player can improve their position by changing strategy.

For Bitcoin nation-state adoption, that point is when enough major countries hold Bitcoin that NOT holding it becomes economically dangerous.

Wave 1 was countries like El Salvador and Bhutan taking real risks for potentially massive rewards. ✓ Done.

Wave 2 is smart followers like the Czech Republic and U.S. states moving while the trend is clear but prices are still reasonable. ← We are here.

Wave 3 will be major powers going full throttle, creating an economic arms race for Bitcoin accumulation.

Wave 4 will be the desperate scramble by countries that waited too long and have to pay whatever price the market demands.

Guess which wave pays $1 million per Bitcoin?

This is what makes million-dollar Bitcoin inevitable...

The Million Dollar Inevitability

Nation-state adoption isn't just another catalyst for Bitcoin reaching a million dollars. It's THE catalyst.

Here's the difference between corporate adoption and government adoption:

- Corporations buy thousands of Bitcoin and maybe hold them for years.
- Governments buy hundreds of thousands of Bitcoin and hold them forever.

When the U.S. Treasury holds Bitcoin alongside gold, when the Czech National Bank allocates 5% of reserves to Bitcoin, when pension funds start rotating into Bitcoin... these aren't trades. These are permanent removals of supply from the market.

The beautiful brutality of fixed supply economics: Every Bitcoin locked away in government reserves is one less Bitcoin available for everyone else.

And everyone else includes every other government that's now realizing they need Bitcoin for their own national security.

So what's next?

What's Next

The nation-state adoption wave isn't coming. It's here. Right now. The only question is which countries will secure their positions before the supply runs out.

America has made their bet. The smart small countries have made theirs. Political leaders like Germany's Lindner, Japan's Hamada, and Brazil's Biondini are desperately trying to wake up their governments before it's too late. The dominoes are falling and fast.

But even this governmental economic race is just setting the stage for something bigger.

Because while countries fight over Bitcoin, the technology itself keeps evolving. The infrastructure keeps improving. The use cases keep expanding.

And when the full potential of Bitcoin's next evolution becomes clear...

Well, that's when million-dollar Bitcoin starts looking conservative.

“The next wave of wealth won’t come from trading—it’ll come from understanding Bitcoin”

Dan Hollings

CHAPTER 7

THE BITCOINIZATION OF FINANCE

When Bitcoin Eats Wall Street (And Asks for Seconds)

> *"Be fearful when others are greedy, and greedy when others are fearful."* —
>
> Warren Buffett

Remember that old video game Kirby? The little pink guy who could inhale enemies and steal their powers?

Yeah, that's Bitcoin right now.

Except instead of eating cartoon monsters, Bitcoin's swallowing entire financial systems... and getting stronger with every bite.

The Great Financial Feast Has Begun

Here's what the "Bitcoin skeptics" got spectacularly wrong:

They thought traditional finance would kill Bitcoin. They thought ETFs would tame it. They thought regulations would neuter it. They thought centralized exchanges would control it.

Instead? Bitcoin did what it does best— absorbed them all. Made them stronger. And kept growing.

It's like watching David not just beat Goliath, but consume Goliath's entire army and use their weapons to conquer the kingdom.

And the best part? We're just getting started.

ETFs: The Day That Changed Everything

January 10th, 2024 was the day Bitcoin spot ETFs were approved in the United States.[1] Bitcoin was trading around $46,000 per coin that day.[2]

We believe that this was the day that The Million Dollar Bitcoin went from being a dream to an inevitability.

Some people speculated this was the day that Bitcoin would fall flat and pass as a fad.

"It didn't"

By December 2024, Bitcoin had broken through $100,000 for the first time in history.[3] The ETFs didn't kill Bitcoin's volatility—they turned Bitcoin into rocket fuel for the entire financial system.

The numbers speak for themselves:

- BlackRock's iShares Bitcoin Trust (IBIT) alone accumulated over $50 billion (yes with a "B") in assets by the end of 2024[4]
- Total Bitcoin ETF inflows exceeded $100 billion in the first year[5]
- IBIT became the most successful ETF launch in history[6]
- Bitcoin's price more than doubled from ETF approval to year-end 2024[7]

But here's the real kicker...

Since ETFs are "regulated products" (fancy Wall Street speak for "the government says it's legit"), you can now borrow against your Bitcoin ETF holdings.

Translation: Your Bitcoin just became legit collateral to use throughout the financial system.

And the interest rates? Lower than your mortgage. Baddabing. Baddaboom!

Old Way vs. Bitcoin Way: Investment Access

Traditional Financial Way	Bitcoin ETF Way
Open brokerage account, wait days for approval	Same day Bitcoin exposure in any retirement account
Deal with private keys, custody, security	Your existing broker handles everything
No borrowing against crypto holdings	Borrow against ETF value at low rates
Separate tax reporting complexity	Standard 1099 forms like any other investment

Bitcoin Mortgages: When Your Digital Gold Buys Real Estate

Here's how this actually works in the real world:

Meet Sarah (based on real customer examples from leading Bitcoin mortgage companies):

Sarah owns 2 Bitcoin worth $200,000. She wants to buy a $100,000 house but doesn't want to sell her Bitcoin and pay capital gains taxes.

Instead, she uses a crypto mortgage company to borrow $100,000 using her Bitcoin as collateral at competitive interest rates. Her Bitcoin stays in secure custody and keeps growing at Bitcoin's historical appreciation rate.

One year later:

- Her 2 Bitcoin are now worth $260,000 (assuming 30% appreciation)
- She owes $104,000 on the loan
- Her net position improved by $56,000
- She owns a house AND her Bitcoin kept appreciating

She literally made money by borrowing money.

This isn't theory. Companies like Milo, Figure, and Ledn are doing this right now with real customers.

The Real Companies Making This Happen Now:

Milo: The Miami-based pioneer that has surpassed $65 million in crypto mortgage volume.[8] Offers 30-year mortgages, up to $5 million using Bitcoin, Ethereum, or USDC as collateral. Minimum $200,000 crypto required. The company has originated over $250 million in total mortgages across all loan products.[9]

Figure: Taking applications for Bitcoin-backed mortgages up to $3 million in select states.

Ledn: Bitcoin-only mortgages, focusing specifically on BTC holders who want to keep their stack intact.

Old Way vs. Bitcoin Way: Real Estate Financing

Traditional Mortgages	Bitcoin Mortgage
20% cash down payment required	0% down (100% financing possible)
Credit checks, income verification, 45-day process	Fast approval based on crypto collateral
Sell investments to fund down payment (triggers taxes)	Keep crypto, avoid capital gains taxes
Limited to traditional income sources	Crypto wealth counts as qualification

But here's the risk you need to know: If Bitcoin crashes dramatically, you might face a margin call requiring more collateral. Most lenders require 100-200% collateralization specifically for this reason.

Bitcoin Life Insurance: Death, Taxes, and Bitcoin Returns

Here's a question that would've sounded insane five years ago:

What if you could pay your life insurance premiums in Bitcoin... and get your payouts in Bitcoin too?

Meet Meanwhile Insurance. The world's first fully regulated life insurance company that operates entirely in Bitcoin.[10] Based in Bermuda and licensed by the Bermuda Monetary Authority, they just did something no company in history has ever done: published audited financial statements denominated entirely in Bitcoin.

Their 2024 numbers are wild:

- Total assets: 220.4 Bitcoin
- Net income: 25.29 Bitcoin (300% year-over-year growth)[11]

They're literally making Bitcoin by running an insurance business.

Now here's why this matters...

Traditional life insurance companies: "Give us your money, we'll grow it at 2-3% annually—maybe."

Meanwhile Insurance: "Pay us in Bitcoin, we'll grow it at Bitcoin rates, you can borrow against it, and your family gets Bitcoin when you die."

How This Actually Works:

Zac Townsend, CEO of Meanwhile, breaks down their most popular policy:

"You pay 1 Bitcoin per year for 10 years. We guarantee a payout of 1.5 Bitcoin to your beneficiaries."[12]

That's it. No complicated formulas. No fine print about dollar conversions.

You pay Bitcoin. Your family gets Bitcoin. Period.

But here's the genius part: After two years, you can borrow against your policy's Bitcoin value at low rates. Tax-free liquidity while your Bitcoin hopefully keeps growing.

Old Way vs. Bitcoin Way: Life Insurance

Traditional Life Insurance	Bitcoin Life Insurance
Premiums paid in dollars	Premiums paid in Bitcoin
2-3% annual policy growth	Bitcoin's historical 30%+ growth
Payouts in depreciating dollars	Payouts in Bitcoin
Complex underwriting, medical exams	Simplified Bitcoin-based approval
Policy loans at high interest rates	Loans against Bitcoin value at low rates

The risk: Bitcoin's volatility means your policy value fluctuates. But Meanwhile's CEO makes a compelling point: "It may feel like the dollar is not as sure a store of value as it might have been in the past. So the idea of storing some value for your kids... in this global, censorship-resistant, decentralized, uncontrollable currency in Bitcoin is very attractive."[13]

Bitcoin Credit Cards: Your Daily Spending Just Got an Upgrade

Here's a wild thought: What if every coffee, every gas fill-up, every grocery run could automatically build your Bitcoin stack?

Welcome to 2025, where your credit card isn't just giving you airline miles (that do not grow in value) anymore. It's giving you Bitcoin.

The New Players in the Game

Coinbase One Card (launching Fall 2025): The heavyweight entering the ring. Up to 4% Bitcoin back on purchases. But here's the kicker—your rewards rate depends on how much crypto you hold with Coinbase. Hold more, earn more.[14]

Gemini Credit Card: Available now in all 50 states. 4% Bitcoin back on gas, 3% on dining, 2% on groceries, 1% on everything else. No annual fee. Instant crypto rewards deposited in real-time.[15] if last year you had $100 in crypto rewards, by the end of the year you would've had $276. It went up 176%. That's something your mIles and points can't do.

Fold Credit Card: The OG Bitcoin rewards card with a waitlist. Offers a flat 2% Bitcoin back for Fold+ subscribers and 1.5% for free users.[16]

Old Way vs. Bitcoin Way: Credit Card Rewards

Traditional Credit Cards	Bitcoin Credit Cards
Earn points/miles that expire or devalue	Earn Bitcoin that appreciates
Complex redemption systems	Automatic instant Bitcoin (and crypto) deposits
1-2% cash back maximum	Up to 4% Bitcoin back
Rewards lose value over time	Rewards potentially gain massive value
Limited redemption options	Bitcoin can be used anywhere or held

Why This Changes Everything

Traditional credit card companies are basically saying: "Here's 1% cash back that buys less every year due to inflation."

Bitcoin credit card companies are saying: "Here's Bitcoin that's averaged significant returns and could hit $1 million per coin."

The math is intriguing: If you spend $50,000 annually and earn 2% Bitcoin back, that's $1,000 in Bitcoin per year. If Bitcoin appreciates significantly, your annual rewards could be worth multiples of their original value.

Getting Started (Your Action Plan):

Start Easy - Bitcoin Credit Cards:

- Apply for Gemini Credit Card (available now, all 50 states)
- Join Coinbase One Card waitlist (launches Fall 2025)
- Zero barriers to entry, immediate Bitcoin accumulation

Level Up - Bitcoin Mortgages:

- Research Milo, Figure, or Ledn
- Minimum typically $200K in crypto
- Expect 100-200% collateralization requirements

Advanced - Bitcoin Life Insurance:

- Meanwhile is currently the only regulated option
- Based in Bermuda, serves global customers
- Minimum policies start around significant premium requirements

The beautiful thing? You don't have to go all-in immediately. Start with a Bitcoin credit card. Use it for your normal spending. Watch your Bitcoin stack grow automatically.

Then, as your comfort level and Bitcoin holdings increase, you can graduate to mortgages and life insurance.

Remember: Start small, understand the risks, and never bet more than you can afford to lose. But also remember—the biggest risk might be waiting too long to get in the Bitcoin game.

What This Means for You (The Real Talk)

Look, we're not going to sugarcoat this. These products are new. They're not for everyone. And yes, there are risks.

But here's what's undeniably happening:

The traditional financial system is organizing itself around Bitcoin. Every month, more companies launch Bitcoin-backed products. Every quarter, more institutions add Bitcoin services.Even banks are getting in on the action.

The early adopters are already leveraging Bitcoin for:

- Mortgages without selling their stack
- Life insurance that grows at Bitcoin rates
- Credit lines against their holdings
- Tax-advantaged wealth transfer
- Daily Bitcoin accumulation through spending

Four types of people are emerging:

1. **The Early Adopters**: Using these products now while they're new and competitive
2. **The Smart Starters**: Beginning with Bitcoin credit cards while learning about the bigger products
3. **The Wait-and-See Crowd**: Watching from the sidelines until it's "proven" (What more proof do they need?)
4. **The Skeptics**: Missing the boat entirely

Which one are you?

The Bottom Line

Traditional finance spent years trying to ignore Bitcoin.

Now traditional finance IS becoming Bitcoin.

Bitcoin doesn't just reach a million dollars in value. Bitcoin becomes the foundation that million-dollar financial strategies are built on.

We're watching the birth of a parallel financial system. One where your house is backed by Bitcoin. Where your life insurance grows at Bitcoin rates. Where your credit comes from your crypto, not your credit score.

The Kirby analogy was perfect: Bitcoin absorbed every attack, gained new powers, and grew stronger.

The financial revolution isn't coming. It's here. NOW.

"Bitcoin isn't a shortcut to wealth, but nonetheless it can get you there"

Dan Hollings

CHAPTER 8

FROM POLLUTION TO PROFIT

The Counterintuitive Story of How Bitcoin Is Revolutionizing The Renewable Industry

"The stone age didn't end because we ran out of stones."

— Sheikh Ahmed Zaki Yamani

February 2021. Winter Storm Uri hit Texas like a freight train nobody saw coming.

Co-author Anthony was boiling water on his gas stove just to stay alive. Co-author Daniel didn't even have that. He was literally flushing his toilet with melted snow.

More than 4.5 million Texans sat in freezing houses for DAYS, wondering how the heck the energy capital of America could fail this hard.[1]

Three years later...

A dangerous heat wave hit Texas except of the power grid failing a Bitcoin mining company was paid $31.7 million in a single month just for agreeing to turn off their computers during the heat wave.[2]

Read that again.

They made nearly FOUR TIMES more money from NOT mining Bitcoin than they did from actually mining Bitcoin just by balancing the grid and turning off their power when necessary.

What. The. Hell.

Welcome to the most counterintuitive energy story you'll ever hear.

The "Grid Balancing" Game: When Doing Nothing Pays Everything

With Winter Storm Uri, the disaster that left millions without power for days, here's what actually happened (and why Bitcoin miners are now the heroes of this story):

The Problem: Power grids need massive capacity during peak demand (like a Texas heat wave or freeze) but way less during normal times. You can't afford to build plants for worst-case scenarios that sit idle 90% of the time, but you also can't let people freeze when emergencies hit.

Traditional Solution: Build expensive "peaker plants" that only run during emergencies. Cost to Texas: $18+ billion in infrastructure.[3]

Bitcoin Solution: Use mining operations as "flexible load" that can instantly turn off when the grid needs power elsewhere.

The Results:

- Texas saved an estimated $18 billion by avoiding the need for traditional peaker plants[4]
- Riot's Rockdale facility created 250 jobs in a town that desperately needed economic revival[5]
- Bitcoin miners can respond to grid emergencies in SECONDS, compared to 10-30 minutes for traditional industrial customers[6]

Old Way vs. Bitcoin Way: Grid Stability

Traditional Grid Management	Bitcoin-Enhanced Grid
Build gas peaker plants: $18+ billion	Use flexible Bitcoin miners: $18 billion saved
10-30 minute response time	Sub-second response time
Fixed capacity, can't scale down	Instantly adjustable load
Burning gas creates emissions	Bitcoin miners create... Bitcoin

The Biggest Energy Revolution in History

Here's a sentence that would've gotten you laughed out of any climate conference five years ago:

"Bitcoin mining is the most cost-effective way to reduce greenhouse gas emissions on the planet."

The math actually checks out.

(We know, we know... our brain exploded too.)

While environmental activists were busy writing Bitcoin's obituary and calling it an "environmental disaster," something INSANE was happening in the real world:

2019: Oil companies flared $750 million worth of natural gas annually in the Permian Basin alone.[7] Just... burned it. For nothing. Creating massive emissions for ZERO economic benefit.

2024: Those same companies are now making millions mining Bitcoin with that "waste" gas while reducing CO2 emissions by 63%.[8]

2020: Renewable energy projects routinely lost money during their "pre-commercial" phase when they generated electricity but weren't connected to the grid yet.

2024: A Cornell study found that 32 planned renewable projects in Texas alone could generate $47 million in profits during this phase by mining Bitcoin.[9]

The numbers are staggering...

But the story behind them? That's what'll blow your mind.

The "Pollution to Profit" Revolution: Real Numbers, Real Impact

Buckle up for this one: turning environmental disasters into Bitcoin goldmines.

Case Study 1: The Two Texas A&M Students Who Made $4 Million from Pollution

Brent Whitehead and Matt Lohstroh were college sophomores watching oil companies burn (or flare) $750 million worth of natural gas every year in the Permian Basin.[10]

Just... burning it. For nothing.

They had this crazy idea: "What if we captured that gas and used it to mine Bitcoin?"

Everyone said they were INSANE.

"Oil companies don't partner with crypto kids." "Environmental waste isn't a business model." "Gas flaring has been happening for 160 years—if there was a solution, someone would've found it."

Blah, blah, blah...

2022 Result: Giga Energy Solutions (their company) made $4 million in their first year, signed deals with 20+ oil and gas companies, and helped reduce emissions by 63% compared to traditional flaring.[11]

The kicker? In some small Texas communities, they became the LARGEST source of revenue, revitalizing "ghost towns" that had been abandoned when traditional energy companies left.

Two college kids just solved a 160-year-old problem... and got rich doing it.

Case Study 2: Riot Platforms' "Million Dollar Days of Doing Nothing"

Riot Platforms operates North America's largest Bitcoin mining facility in Rockdale, Texas. It uses enough electricity to power 300,000 homes.[12]

Here's where it gets WEIRD:

July 2023: Riot mined 410 BTC and made $7.8 million in energy credits.

August 2023: During a record-breaking heat wave, Riot mined 333 BTC (19% less) but made $31.7 million in energy credits (4x more).[13]

Read that again.

They mined LESS Bitcoin but made FOUR TIMES more money from energy credits by voluntarily shutting down during peak demand periods.

(We had to read this three times myself...)

The math: By mining 19% fewer Bitcoin, they earned an extra $23.9 million in energy credits compared to the previous month.

But here's the beautiful irony...

Bitcoin miners actually WANT to get these shutdown requests because the grid often pays them more than they'd make mining. They've built a business model around being the grid's emergency relief valve.

It's like getting paid MORE to not work than to work. (Where do we sign up?)

Case Study 3: The Renewable Energy Moonshot

A 2023 Cornell study analyzed planned renewable energy projects across the U.S. and found that projects in Texas could turn a massive profit from Bitcoin mining during their pre-commercial phase.[14]

Texas standouts:

- Aktina Solar Project (250 MW): $3.23 million in potential Bitcoin mining profits
- Roseland Solar Project (250 MW): $3.23 million in potential profits

- Western Trail Wind Project (367 MW): $2.65 million in potential profits

The bigger picture: 32 planned renewable projects in Texas could generate combined profits of $47 million using Bitcoin mining during development.[15]

One study found that integrating Bitcoin mining reduced a solar project's payback period from 8.1 years to 3.5 years.[16]

Yeah... Bitcoin just made solar energy pay for itself in HALF the time.

The Methane Capture Miracle: Turning Climate Poison into Digital Gold

Here's where the environmental story goes into even stranger territory.

Methane is 84 times more potent than CO2 at trapping heat over 20 years.[17] The U.S. oil and gas industry is one of the world's top gas flaring countries, right behind Russia, Iran, and Iraq.

(Not exactly the company you want to keep...)

In the Permian Basin alone, roughly $750 million worth of gas gets wasted each year through flaring.[18] That's three-quarters of a billion dollars of energy literally burned and thrown away annually.

Let me repeat that: $750 MILLION... just burned... for nothing.

Traditional flaring efficiency: 91.1% of methane gets destroyed, but 8.9% still escapes as pure methane (which is exceedingly bad for the environment).[19]

Bitcoin mining efficiency: 99.89% of methane gets combusted, with virtually zero methane escape[20]

Environmental impact: 63% reduction in CO2-equivalent emissions compared to continued flaring[21]

The Real-World Impact: Before and After

Before Bitcoin Mining (2019):

- Wesco Operating: Flaring 240,000 SCF of gas per day
- Environmental cost: Massive methane emissions
- Economic benefit: $0 (actually negative due to flaring equipment costs)

After Bitcoin Mining (2022):

- Wesco Operating: Flaring reduced to 0 SCF per day
- Environmental benefit: 63% reduction in emissions
- Economic benefit: New revenue stream from Bitcoin mining

Giga Energy (founded by those Texas A&M students) now has deals with 20+ oil and gas companies and is expanding rapidly.[22]

Crusoe Energy now operates 140+ Bitcoin mines across North America, helping major producers like ExxonMobil and Equinor reduce flaring.[23]

Two college kids started a revolution that's now helping Fortune 500 companies save the planet while making money.

The Numbers That Prove Bitcoin Is the Ultimate Climate Solution

Per megawatt capacity installed, Bitcoin mining for methane mitigation provides 9,482 tons of CO2 equivalent emissions reduction annually.[24]

Compare that to:

- Wind power: 1,917 tons of CO2 reduction per megawatt
- Solar power: 1,278 tons of CO2 reduction per megawatt

Bitcoin mining is 5x more effective than wind and 7x more effective than solar at reducing greenhouse gas emissions per megawatt installed.

But wait... there's more.

(We sound like a late-night infomercial, but the data keeps getting crazier.)

The Renewable Energy Accelerator

While critics were complaining about Bitcoin's energy use, miners were quietly becoming the renewable energy industry's best customer.

The Renewable Energy Paradox: Solar peaks at noon when demand is low. Wind blows strongest at night when everyone's asleep. This "excess" energy often gets sold at a loss or simply wasted.

Bitcoin's Solution: Buy that excess energy 24/7 at any price.

Study Results from Texas:

- Solar capacity increased by 20% when Bitcoin mining was added with demand response
- Wind capacity EXPLODED by 142%
- Gas peaker plants were completely eliminated
- Price volatility decreased for all consumers[25]

Real Company Examples:

- CleanSpark: Gets 94% of power from carbon-free sources (nuclear, hydro, wind, solar)[26]
- Gryphon Digital Mining: 100% renewable power, publishes full emissions data, links executive pay to sustainability goals[27]
- MARA: Just acquired a 114 MW wind farm to build power demand locally and reduce grid congestion[28]

The Skeptics' Questions (And the Counterintuitive Answers)

"But what if Bitcoin crashes? Won't this whole system collapse?"

This is the beautiful part: When Bitcoin prices are low, miners actually have MORE incentive to shut down during peak demand periods because the grid payments exceed mining profits.

As one expert put it: "If the price of Bitcoin is fairly low, then there's more incentive to turn off [their computers] in peak demand or in extreme weather."[29]

The system is MORE stable when Bitcoin is volatile, not less.

"Won't governments just ban this?"

Too late.

States like Texas, Wyoming, Montana, and Pennsylvania are offering tax breaks to attract Bitcoin miners specifically for grid stabilization and methane reduction.

Even Senator Ted Cruz calls Bitcoin miners essential for grid reliability because they can "turn off all of their machines with a few seconds' notice when the grid is in a pinch."[30]

Future Scenario: Picture This...

It's 2028. Bitcoin is at $800,000. Here's what a typical day looks like:

6 AM: Solar farms across the Southwest start producing excess electricity. Instead of wasting production, they automatically route power to co-located Bitcoin mining containers, generating revenue during off-peak hours.

12 PM: An unexpected equipment failure takes a power plant offline in Texas. Within SECONDS, 50+ Bitcoin mining operations across the state automatically shut down, instantly returning 2,000 MW to the grid—enough to power 1.6 million homes.

3 PM: A wind farm in Wyoming that would've been economically unviable just broke ground, fully funded by a 5-year Bitcoin mining revenue guarantee during the development phase.

8 PM: An oil well in North Dakota that would've flared $50,000 worth of gas this month instead generates $50,000 worth of Bitcoin while reducing emissions by 63%.

11 PM: ERCOT (runs the Texas power grid) sends out payments to demand response participants. Bitcoin miners earn more in credits than they would've made mining. The grid stays stable. Residents' power bills stay low.

The energy currency of the world isn't the dollar anymore.

It's Bitcoin.

The DePIN/DeSci Connection: Energy Infrastructure Enables Everything

Bitcoin's energy revolution isn't happening in isolation. When you create financial incentives powerful enough to make renewable energy profitable in remote locations, you unlock opportunities far beyond electricity:

Decentralized Physical Infrastructure Networks (DePIN): Those same Bitcoin mining operations that stabilize power grids can also host cellular towers, internet relays, and sensor networks. Volcano Energy in El Salvador is developing a 241-megawatt renewable energy park specifically to power Bitcoin mining and infrastructure—creating the foundation for an entire digital economy.[31]

Decentralized Science (DeSci): When renewable energy becomes profitable anywhere on Earth thanks to Bitcoin mining, researchers can fund and operate remote sensing stations, climate monitoring equipment, and distributed computing networks without waiting for government grants or university approval.

The pattern is clear: Bitcoin doesn't just monetize energy.

It monetizes the infrastructure that energy makes possible.

The Million Dollar Question

When Bitcoin reaches $1 million, it won't be because of speculation or adoption alone.

It'll be because Bitcoin has become the energy coordination mechanism of the world—the thing that makes wind farms profitable, turns environmental problems into profit centers, unlocks stranded energy sources, and provides the economic foundation for humanity's transition to abundant, clean energy.

We're not just watching number go up.

We're watching the birth of Energy Bitcoin—a world where:

- Renewable energy projects can achieve profitability during development phases instead of waiting years for grid connections
- Environmental waste becomes the most cost-effective way to reduce greenhouse gas emissions
- Grid stability pays better than traditional energy production
- Ocean thermal energy, geothermal systems, and other "impossible" renewable technologies suddenly become economically viable because they have a guaranteed customer who'll buy energy 24/7 at any location

The Bottom Line

Traditional energy companies spent years trying to paint Bitcoin as an environmental disaster.

Now they're all mining Bitcoin and discovering it's the best thing that ever happened to their environmental impact reports.

The governments that banned Bitcoin mining are now competing to attract Bitcoin miners for methane reduction and grid stabilization.

The environmental activists who called Bitcoin a climate catastrophe are watching it become the most powerful tool for accelerating the renewable energy transition in history.

The transformation is already measurable:

- $47 million in renewable energy development funding in Texas alone
- $18 billion saved in Texas grid infrastructure
- 63% reduction in methane emissions from oil operations
- 142% increase in wind capacity where Bitcoin mining is deployed

Bitcoin doesn't just hit $1 million because people want it.

Bitcoin hits $1 million because the planet NEEDS it to coordinate the transition to clean, abundant energy.

And if you're holding Bitcoin while this transformation happens...

Well, your future self is going to send you a very energy-efficient, carbon-negative thank-you note.

(You can thank me later.)

“Want to be a millionaire? Step one: own one Bitcoin. Step two: don’t flinch.”

Dan Hollings

CHAPTER 9

HOW TO ACTUALLY PROFIT FROM BITCOIN (WITHOUT LOSING YOUR SHIRT)

"The best investment is the one you can sleep through."

— Anonymous Bitcoin Millionaire

IMPORTANT RISK DISCLOSURE: All investing involves substantial risk, including the potential loss of principal. Bitcoin is an extremely volatile asset, and you could lose 100% of your investment. Only invest what you can afford to lose completely. Past performance does not guarantee future results. This is educational content only - we are not licensed financial advisors and this is not financial advice. Consult with a qualified financial advisor before making any investment decisions.

Okay, so at this point you get it…

Bitcoin is a financial revolution on many levels.

And if our thesis is correct—if Bitcoin really is headed to $1 million per coin, as predicted by numerous experts—then understanding how to profit from this historic wealth transfer isn't just smart…

It's absolutely critical.

Because here's the thing everybody really wants to know: How the heck do you actually make money from this thing WITHOUT getting destroyed by the volatility?

Understanding Bitcoin's awesome potential is one thing…

Timing your entry and positioning yourself to capture life-changing gains on the way to $1 million?

That's where most people mess it up spectacularly.

(Including us, by the way. More on that later...)

The truth is, there are five primary ways to profit from Bitcoin's march to $1 million. Some are dead simple. Others require you to develop the emotional discipline of a Tibetan monk and the analytical skills of a NASA engineer.

We're going to walk through all of them—from the "so simple a 10 year old could do it" strategies to the "this might stress-test your marriage but could also change your family's financial future forever" approaches.

Ready?

Let's dive into how to turn Bitcoin knowledge into actual wealth as it climbs toward that million-dollar milestone...

Strategy #1: HODL (aka "The Million-Dollar Patience Play")

First, let us explain what "HODL" means because it's the foundation of every Bitcoin millionaire's strategy…

HODL started as a typo. Back in December 2013, a drunk user named GameKyuubi on the BitcoinTalk forum tried to type "HOLD" but his fingers betrayed him. Instead of deleting it, he posted: "I AM HODLING."[1]

The crypto community loved it so much that it became the unofficial motto of long-term Bitcoin believers.

And here's the beautiful part: HODLing is literally the most successful investment strategy in Bitcoin history—and a great approach for riding Bitcoin to $1 million.

Let's look at some real numbers. If you had bought Bitcoin at almost any point in its history and held for at least four years, you would have profited. According to current data, Bitcoin closing prices show dramatic appreciation over time periods:

- 1 Year Ago: Up 87.1%
- 2 Years Ago: Up 382%
- 3 Years Ago: Up 67.3% (even through the bear market)
- 4 Years Ago: Up 194.7%
- 5 Years Ago: Up 988%[2]

The pattern is clear: Every single person who has bought Bitcoin and held it for at least four years has profited, no matter the purchase price.

EVERY. SINGLE. PERSON.

Now imagine what happens if and when Bitcoin hits our $1 million price target...

If you buy Bitcoin today at around $100,000 and we're right about the million-dollar thesis, that's a 10x return. Your $10,000 becomes $100,000. Your $50,000 becomes $500,000.

The HODLing strategy for the million-dollar Bitcoin is stupidly simple:

1. Open a crypto exchange account (like Coinbase. Binance, etc.)
2. Buy Bitcoin (easy as buying on Amazon)
3. Once you've got more than a few hundred bucks in Bitcoin, move it to a cold wallet (hardware wallet)
4. Forget you own it for the next 5-10 years
5. Check back when Bitcoin hits $1 million and buy whatever you want

That's it.

No daily chart watching. No stress-induced ulcers. No trying to time the market. Just... wait for the inevitable.

But here's the catch: HODLing requires you to have the emotional fortitude to watch your investment drop 50-80% during bear markets and not panic sell.

Most people can't do it.

(Fun fact in the School of Hard Knocks: We know a guy who bought $5,000 worth of Bitcoin in 2017 at $19,000. When it crashed to $3,200 in 2018, he panic-sold—losing 83% of his investment. If he'd just HODLed, that investment would be worth over $26,000 today. Instead, he bought a very expensive lesson in emotional discipline.)

The million-dollar question: Can you hold through a crash believing Bitcoin is destined for $1 million?

Strategy #2: DCA (Dollar-Cost Averaging) - "The Millionaire's Tortoise Strategy"

Dollar-Cost Averaging was first popularized by Benjamin Graham in his book *The Intelligent Investor*. You might know Graham's most famous protégé: Warren Buffett.

So yeah, this strategy has stood the test of time.

The concept is dead simple: Instead of trying to time the market, you buy a fixed dollar amount of Bitcoin on a regular schedule—weekly, monthly, whatever—regardless of the price.

When Bitcoin is expensive, you get fewer sats (a "satoshi" - often abbreviated as "sat" or "sats"- is the smallest unit of Bitcoin). When it's cheap, you get more sats. Over time, this smooths out the short-term volatility while still capturing Bitcoin's long-term trajectory toward $1 million.

Real-world DCA results are impressive. According to crypto DCA analysis, a systematic investment approach has historically outperformed trying to time the market. Studies show that DCA strategies help reduce the impact of volatility while still capturing long-term gains.[3]

Now imagine continuing this strategy as Bitcoin climbs from $100,000 to $1 million over the next decade...

If you DCA $100 per week starting today at $100,000 Bitcoin, and Bitcoin reaches $1 million in 8 years, your weekly purchases near the beginning would see 10x gains, while your later purchases would see smaller but still substantial returns.

The beauty of DCA on the way to $1 million Bitcoin: You're automatically buying more Bitcoin when it's cheaper and less when it's expensive, positioning yourself to capture maximum gains as it reaches our price target.

Warren Buffett himself supports dollar cost averaging: "If you like spending six to eight hours per week working on investments, do it. If you don't, then dollar-cost average into index funds."[4]

Replace "index funds" with "Bitcoin on its way to $1 million" and you've got the strategy that's created more crypto millionaires than any other approach.

DCA works because it forces you to buy consistently, removes emotion from the equation, and protects you from the biggest killer of investment returns: trying to time the market on Bitcoin's volatile journey to seven figures.

Strategy #3: Buy During Bear Markets (aka "The Millionaire's Secret Weapon")

This is where things get psychologically difficult...

Bear markets are when Bitcoin drops 50-80% from its peak and everyone declares it "dead" for the 500th time. The media writes obituaries. Your family questions your sanity. Even crypto bros start quietly updating their LinkedIn profiles.

But here's the thing about bear markets: They're where many Bitcoin millionaires are made.

During the 2022 crypto winter, Bitcoin dropped from approximately $69,000 to around $15,500. The headlines were brutal:

- "Crypto Is Dead"
- "The Bitcoin Experiment Has Failed"
- "Time to Admit Crypto Was Just a Bubble"

But smart money? Smart money was buying with both hands.

If you had bought Bitcoin during that bear market bottom in late 2022 and held until it crossed $100,000 in December 2024, you'd be sitting on substantial gains in just about two years.[5]

Now imagine what happens during the next bear market on Bitcoin's way to $1 million...

If Bitcoin pulls back 60-70% like it has historically done from whatever peak it hits next (maybe $126,000+?), that will likely be your last chance to accumulate Bitcoin below six figures before the final push to $1 million.

The problem is that buying during bear markets requires you to act when every fiber of your being is screaming "RUN AWAY!"

This is what separates future Bitcoin millionaires from the crowd: the ability to buy when everyone else is selling.

Bear markets are when assets go on sale. But most people only want to buy when prices are going up (which is exactly backwards for building wealth).

As Baron Nathan Rothschild reportedly said: "Buy when there's blood in the streets, even if the blood is your own."

Bear markets are when others are fearful. That's your cue to be greedy and position yourself for Bitcoin's potential climb to $1 million.

Strategy #4: The Indicators Game (For Those Who Want To Time The Million-Dollar Journey)

Alright, this is where we get into the fun stuff...

While HODL and DCA are "set it and forget it" strategies, some people want more granular control over their buying and selling as Bitcoin makes its way to $1 million. They want indicators, charts, and signals to help them make better-informed decisions.

We're going to share two ridiculously simple indicators that can help you buy low and sell high on Bitcoin's journey to seven figures. But remember: There's no such thing as a perfect indicator. These are tools to help you make better decisions, not crystal balls.

The Bitcoin Rainbow Chart

The Bitcoin Rainbow Chart is basically a color-coded "buy/sell/hold" signal for Bitcoin that's been surprisingly accurate over the years.[6]

Reading it is stupidly simple:

- **Bottom colors (blue, purple):** Bitcoin is cheap. Buy time.
- **Middle colors (green, yellow):** Bitcoin is fairly valued. HODL time.
- **Top colors (orange, red):** Bitcoin is expensive. Consider taking profits.

The first Bitcoin Rainbow Chart was created by a Bitcoin Talk user called "trolololo" in 2014 when Bitcoin was much lower in price. The chart has been updated several times to maintain accuracy, but the core concept remains the same.[7]

Here's the beautiful part: The chart even has a purple band labeled "Bitcoin is dead" for when the price dips below the blue band. Historically, when Bitcoin hit these extreme low zones, buyers would see substantial gains in the following periods.

But here's the psychological challenge: When Bitcoin is in the blue or purple bands, that's when FUD (Fear, Uncertainty, Doubt) is highest. That's when your family thinks you're insane for buying more. That's when the media is writing Bitcoin's obituary.

But historically, those have been the most profitable times to position yourself for Bitcoin's next leg up toward $1 million.

Important note: The Rainbow Chart is considered a meme chart created for entertainment. It is not investment advice and should not be taken too seriously. But as meme charts go, it's been surprisingly useful for understanding long-term trends over Bitcoin's history.[8]

The Crypto Fear & Greed Index

The crypto fear & greed index provides an easy overview of the current sentiment of the Bitcoin/crypto market at a glance. Each day, analysts analyze emotions and sentiments from different sources and crunch them into one simple number from 0 to 100.[9]

Here's how it breaks down:

- 0-24: Extreme Fear
- 25-49: Fear
- 50-74: Greed
- 75-100: Extreme Greed

The logic is Warren Buffett simple:

- When the market is fearful (low numbers), people are selling in droves, often creating buying opportunities for Bitcoin's climb to $1 million
- When the market is greedy (high numbers), people are buying like crazy, often creating profit-taking opportunities

Research shows the Fear and Greed Index has been "mildly correlated" with Bitcoin price movements. Studies indicate that extreme values of fear have often led to bullish trend reversals, while extreme values of greed have led to milder reactions.[10]

The beautiful thing about the Fear & Greed Index is that it gives you permission to buy when everyone else thinks you're crazy—exactly the positioning you want for Bitcoin's journey to $1 million.

When the index is showing "Extreme Fear," that's often code for "Bitcoin is on sale before its next move higher."

Strategy #5: The Midas Method - Automated, All-Weather Bitcoin Profits (For Those Who Want Monthly Income on the Way to $1 Million)

Okay, this is where you get ease and effectiveness.

Most people think they have to choose between two approaches for Bitcoin's climb to $1 million:

Hold and pray - Buy Bitcoin and wait 5-10 years for it to hit $1 million (but generate zero income along the way)

Trade manually - Try to time the ups and downs to generate regular profits (but likely lose money due to emotions and bad timing)

But what if there was another option?

What if you could generate consistent monthly income from Bitcoin's volatility WHILE still potentially positioning yourself for long-term gains on the journey to $1 million?

Enter The Midas Method: Your AI robotic trading assistant that turns Bitcoin's daily price movements into regular profits.

The Brutal Reality of Manual Trading

Most people think active trading is the holy grail of Bitcoin profits. You know—buying and selling based on charts, indicators, and "market timing" to maximize gains on Bitcoin's way to $1 million.

And they're right about one thing: Active trading CAN be incredibly profitable.

But here's what nobody tells you about trying to time Bitcoin markets manually:

- 80-90% of day traders lose money over time (study after study confirms this)[11]
- You're competing against algorithms that process information in milliseconds
- One emotional decision can wipe out months of gains
- The stress literally ages you—sleepless nights, constant chart watching, relationship strain
- FOMO and revenge trading destroy even experienced traders
- The market is open 24/7, but you need sleep (Bitcoin doesn't)

Multiple academic studies consistently show that the vast majority of day traders lose money. A comprehensive study of Brazilian day traders found that only 3% were profitable, with just 1.1% earning above minimum wage.[12] Another study of Taiwanese day traders over 15 years showed that only about 1% of day traders were able to consistently profit.[13]

We've watched brilliant people lose fortunes because they couldn't stick to their own rules. They'd have perfect entry and exit strategies written down, then throw it all away the moment Bitcoin started mooning or crashing.

Here's the thing about emotions and money: They don't mix well.

When you're manually trading, you're fighting millions of years of human evolution. Fear and greed aren't bugs in your operating system—they're features designed to keep you alive in the wild. But they're absolute poison in financial markets.

The Midas Method: Truly Passive Income While Bitcoin Climbs

A few years back, our co-author Dan Hollings cracked the code on something extraordinary: an automated Bitcoin trading system that removes human emotion from the equation entirely. We call it The Plan (ThePlan-Programs.com).

And under The Plan's umbrella of automated trading strategies, The Midas Method stands out. It's basically like having a tireless robot trader that follows systematic rules 24/7 without ever getting scared, greedy, grouchy, or tired.

The best part? **The Midas Method is designed for complete beginners.** You don't need:

- Prior trading experience
- Technical analysis skills
- Advanced computer knowledge
- To understand complex charts or indicators

If you can navigate a website and follow step-by-step instructions, you can run this system. The bot handles all the complex buying and selling automatically—you're simply setting it up and letting it run.

This wasn't something we threw together over a weekend. The Midas Method represents years of development, millions of dollars in research and testing, and countless hours of backtesting across every market condition imaginable. We analyzed tons of market data, tested thousands of scenarios, and refined the algorithms through bear and bull markets to create a system that could handle whatever the crypto markets throw at it.

Here's how it works:

Instead of you staring at charts all day trying to time the market, the Midas Method uses proprietary "Golden Touch" settings to automatically buy and sell Bitcoin in small increments as the price moves up and down.

It's not trying to catch massive swings or predict the future. It's simply capturing the natural volatility that happens every single day in Bitcoin markets—volatility that most people see as "noise" but the system turns into consistent profits.

The Results During Testing:

During backtesting across major exchanges, the Midas Method generated:

- 31.29% annual returns on Coinbase
- 46.53% annual returns on KuCoin
- 48.48% annual returns on Binance

Past performance does not guarantee future results. Backtesting results may not reflect actual trading conditions.

That's more than double Warren Buffett's legendary 20% annual returns, achieved automatically while you live your life.

But here's where it gets interesting for Bitcoin's million-dollar journey:

- When Bitcoin crashed 20% during global market turmoil (while manual traders were panic-selling), the Midas Method made 12.34%.
- During those boring sideways months when HODLers watched their portfolios flatline, Midas generated 14.34%.

The system literally profits whether Bitcoin goes up, down, or sideways on its way to $1 million. It's like having a money-making machine that turns market chaos into your personal payday.

Why This Changes Everything for Bitcoin Millionaires

Think about the fundamental problem we've been discussing throughout this chapter: most Bitcoin investment strategies force you to choose between growth and income.

HODLing? You might see massive gains when Bitcoin hits $1 million, but you're like a farmer sitting on valuable land with no cash flow. Your bills don't stop while you hopefully wait for that one big payday years in the future.

DCA and indicator-based buying? Better than HODLing for managing volatility, but you're still not generating regular income from your Bitcoin position.

Manual trading? Sure, you can generate income, but at the cost of your sanity, sleep, and probably your relationships.

The Midas Method offers a different approach: you can generate regular income from Bitcoin's volatility as it climbs toward $1 million.

Think about it:

- Monthly paydays while Bitcoin climbs
- Works in all market conditions (up, down, sideways)
- No chart watching or sleepless nights
- No emotional decisions to ruin your returns
- Runs 24/7 while you focus on your life
- Truly passive income—the bot does all the work

The Growth vs. Income Trade-Off: What You Need to Know

Here's the honest truth about how The Midas Method works—and why understanding this matters for your Bitcoin million-dollar strategy:

When the bot captures profits from Bitcoin's volatility, it extracts those gains as income you can withdraw. Here's a simple example: If you invest $1,000 and the bot sells at a 2.5% profit, you now have $1,025 available. That $25 becomes your passive income, and the bot reinvests the original $1,000 in the next trading cycle.

This means your principal stays constant unless you actively choose to reinvest your profits back into the system.

So if Bitcoin climbs from $100,000 to $1 million while you're running the Midas Method with a fixed principal, you're extracting regular income the entire way up, but your principal doesn't automatically grow 10x like it would with pure HODLing.

This is the fundamental trade-off:

- **Pure HODLing** = Maximum price appreciation potential with zero income along the way
- **Midas Method (fixed principal)** = Regular monthly income but stable principal
- **The Midas Multiplier** = The sweet spot between both strategies

Introducing: The Midas Multiplier Strategy

There's a powerful middle ground called "The Midas Multiplier"—where you reinvest a percentage of your profits back into the system instead of withdrawing everything.

This creates compounding returns that give you BOTH regular income AND growing principal as Bitcoin climbs toward $1 million.

Here's how it works: Let's say you're in the 25% tax bracket. The optimal strategy is to reinvest approximately 50% of your profits back into your principal while withdrawing the other 50% as income. This way:

- You're generating regular cash flow you can use today
- Your principal is growing through reinvestment
- You're optimizing for tax efficiency
- You're capturing compound growth as Bitcoin rises

It's not quite the full 10x growth of pure HODLing from $100,000 to $1 million, but it's consistent income PLUS compound growth—and for many people positioning for Bitcoin's million-dollar journey, that's the perfect balance.

You get to pay your bills today while your Bitcoin position grows for tomorrow.

Ready to Learn More About The Midas Method?

The Midas Method isn't always available. Dan and our team only open enrollment periodically for intensive training sessions.

Why? Because we provide detailed education and support to make sure every participant—regardless of experience level—understands the system completely. You get access to comprehensive training that walks you through the entire approach, from absolute basics to advanced optimization.

Before you risk a single dollar, you'll practice in demo mode with virtual money, watching the system work in real-time without any financial risk.

You'll see the bot make trades, capture profits, and operate across different market conditions—all with zero money on the line.

Here's the kicker: The Plan trading strategies have over 20,000 participants from 150+ countries—many of whom started as complete beginners with zero trading experience.

You could say The Plan is catching on among crypto investors positioning for Bitcoin's rise to $1 million.

Want to Be Notified When The Midas Method Opens Again?

If you want the potential for regular income as Bitcoin climbs toward $1 million, or you want to explore strategies beyond pure HODLing without the stress of manual trading, you can join the waiting list for our next introduction training:

Get on The Midas Method Waiting List → https://theplan.link/midasworthy

Or scan →	

You'll be the first to know when the next enrollment window opens, plus you'll get exclusive access to case studies showing exactly how the system works—including real examples of The Midas Multiplier strategy in action.

Important Tax Considerations

Before we wrap up, let's talk about something most Bitcoin education ignores: taxes.

Every Bitcoin transaction is potentially a taxable event in most countries. This includes:

- Selling Bitcoin for fiat currency
- Trading Bitcoin for other cryptocurrencies
- Using Bitcoin to purchase goods or services
- Receiving Bitcoin from automated trading systems

If you're using any active strategy (especially automated trading), you'll likely have multiple taxable events throughout the year. In the United States, these could be subject to either short-term capital gains (taxed as ordinary income) or long-term capital gains (preferential tax rates for assets held over one year).

Our recommendation: Consult with a crypto-savvy tax professional BEFORE implementing any Bitcoin strategy. The tax implications could significantly impact your overall returns, and proper planning can help you keep more of your Bitcoin gains as it climbs toward $1 million.

Good recordkeeping is essential. Consider using crypto tax software to track all transactions automatically.

Remember: The goal is to build wealth, not to hand it all over to the tax authorities due to poor planning.

The Psychological Warfare of Bitcoin Investing

Here's what nobody tells you about investing in Bitcoin on its way to $1 million…

The biggest enemy isn't market volatility. It's not regulation. It's not even technical analysis.

It's YOU.

Your emotions. Your fear. Your greed. Your inability to stick to the plan when things get uncomfortable.

We've watched people:

- Panic sell at the bottom of bear markets
- FOMO buy at the top of bull markets
- Change strategies every week based on the latest YouTube video
- Risk money they couldn't afford to lose
- Forget their wallet passwords (this is more common than you think)
- Put it all into a meme coin that went to zero
- Ruminate over the "woulda, could, shoulda's"

The most successful Bitcoin investors we know aren't the smartest. They're not the ones with the best technical analysis. They're the ones with the best emotional discipline.

They buy during bear markets when everyone thinks they're crazy.

They hold through 50-80% drawdowns when their friends think they've lost their minds.

They take some profits during euphoric bull markets when everyone thinks Bitcoin will go to $10 million next week.

The market is designed to separate you from your money through emotional manipulation. Your job is to not let it shake you out before Bitcoin reaches $1 million.

The Bottom Line: Choose Your Path to Bitcoin's $1 Million Target

Look, here's the truth about positioning yourself for Bitcoin's climb to $1 million...

If you want simplicity: HODL or DCA. Buy Bitcoin, put it in a hardware wallet, and check back when it hits $1 million. This has historically been the most profitable approach with the least stress.

If you want more control: Use the Rainbow Chart and Fear & Greed Index to time your entries and exits. Buy when others are fearful, take some profits when others are greedy.

If you want income plus potential growth: The Midas Method has an option we call The Midas Multiplier which is designed to compound returns and gives you the potential for monthly profits through automation while maintaining your position for Bitcoin's climb to $1 million.

If you're a glutton for punishment: Develop a systematic manual trading plan and stick to it religiously. But understand that this path is littered with failed traders who couldn't control their emotions.

The strategy you choose depends on your risk tolerance, time commitment, goals, and emotional constitution.

But here's what all successful Bitcoin investors have in common:

They started. They didn't wait for the "perfect" moment or until they understood everything. They got skin in the game.

They stayed consistent. Whether through learning, regular DCA purchases, systematic trading rules, or automated systems, they stuck to their plan through the ups and downs.

They didn't let short-term volatility scare them away from long-term opportunity. They understood that Bitcoin's path to $1 million won't be a straight line—and they positioned themselves accordingly.

The worst thing you can do is analysis paralysis. Pick a strategy that matches your personality and risk tolerance, then execute it consistently.

Because while we're sitting here debating investment strategies, Bitcoin is busy becoming the foundation of the world's new digital economy.

And when that transformation is complete…

When Bitcoin becomes so essential to global infrastructure that $1 million per coin seems conservative…

Well, let's just say you'll want to already be holding your position.

Your future millionaire self will thank you.

Ready to learn more about generating income on Bitcoin's way to $1 million?

Get on The Midas Method Waiting List → https://theplan.link/midasworthy

Get notified about our next introduction training and discover how to potentially profit from Bitcoin's volatility while positioning for the million-dollar target.

Next up: Chapter 10, is Bitcoin risky?

"You don't need a PhD to understand Bitcoin.
Just a little foresight."

Dan Hollings

CHAPTER 10

IS BITCOIN RISKY? (THE BRUTALLY HONEST TRUTH)

"The biggest risk in Bitcoin isn't volatility. It's not regulations. It's not even quantum computers. The biggest risk... is you."

— Some Bitcoin Veteran Who Lost Everything Because He Forgot His Password

Picture this...

It's a quiet Sunday morning in Newport, Wales. James Howells is frantically searching through his house, turning over couch cushions, emptying drawers, checking every possible hiding spot.

He's looking for something worth over $900 million.

A hard drive. A tiny piece of metal and plastic that contains the keys to 8,000 Bitcoin he mined back when most people thought cryptocurrency was just internet funny money.

The problem?

It's not in his house. It's not anywhere.

Four years earlier, during a routine office cleanup, James accidentally threw that hard drive in the trash. His then-girlfriend took the garbage bag to the local dump, not knowing she was tossing away what would become one of the most expensive mistakes in human history.

Today, those 8,000 coins sit somewhere under thousands of tons of rotting garbage in a Welsh landfill. James has spent over a decade trying to convince the local council to let him dig up the entire dump. They keep saying no.

In January 2025, a British High Court judge struck down his latest legal attempt, ruling his case had "no reasonable chance of success." But James isn't giving up. His latest plan? Tokenizing his claim to the lost Bitcoin and trying to buy the dump itself.

(Talk about expensive life lessons...)

Now, why are we starting a chapter about Bitcoin risks with this story?

Because after spending nine chapters convincing you that Bitcoin is headed to $1 million, we'd be doing you a massive disservice if we didn't also tell you about the ways this whole thing could go sideways.

And James Howells represents the most important lesson in all of Bitcoin investing:

At this point in the life of Bitcoin the biggest enemy isn't market crashes, government regulations, or technical failures. One of the biggest enemies is human error.

So let's dive into the real risks that could separate you from your Bitcoin millions... and more importantly, how to avoid becoming the next cautionary tale.

The #1 Risk: YOU (And Your Terrible Human Habits)

Let us be brutally honest about something…

According to the FBI's 2024 Internet Crime Report, Americans lost $9.3 billion to cryptocurrency fraud alone—that's out of $16.6 billion total cybercrime losses, up 33% from the year before.[1]

But here's the kicker: A huge chunk of these "thefts" weren't sophisticated Ocean's Eleven-style heists. They were people doing incredibly dumb things with their Bitcoin.

Here's where Bitcoin gets tricky for newcomers...

If you already understand the differences between hot wallets and cold wallets, and know what seed phrases are all about, you can skip this section and jump to "DON'T BE THIS GUY" below.

For everyone else, let's do a quick Bitcoin Security 101:

What's a Private Key? Think of your private key as the deed to your digital house. It's a super-long password (usually 64 random characters) that proves you own your Bitcoin. Lose the deed, lose the house. No customer service department. No "I forgot my password" button. No do-overs. Just... gone forever.

What's a Seed Phrase? A seed phrase is your private key written in human-friendly words instead of random characters. It's usually 12 or 24 words like "apple bicycle mountain thunder..." This phrase can recreate your private key, so it's basically a backup to your backup.

Hot Wallet vs. Cold Wallet - What's the Difference?

Hot Wallet: Connected to the internet (like apps on your phone or browser extensions). Convenient but vulnerable to hackers.

Cold Wallet: Offline storage (like a hardware device or paper). Less convenient but much more secure.

Think of it like this: Hot wallets are like carrying cash in your pocket—great for spending, risky for life savings. Cold wallets are like a bank vault—harder to access, but way safer for large amounts.

Now that we've covered the basics...

DON'T BE THIS GUY: The Social Engineering Victim

Meet Mike (not his real name, but this definitely happened)...

Mike gets a call from someone claiming to be from Coinbase security. They say there's been "suspicious activity" on his account. They need him to "verify" his credentials by logging into this totally-legit-looking website they'll text him.

Quick pause: Coinbase is one of the largest cryptocurrency exchanges where people buy and sell Bitcoin. Think of it like a digital bank for crypto.

The fake website looks exactly like the real Coinbase. Same logo, same colors, same layout. Mike enters his username and password.

Within hours, his Bitcoin is gone. Forever.

The "customer service" number? Fake. The website? A perfect copy designed to steal credentials. Mike? Just another victim of what security experts call social engineering.

QUICK SECURITY CHECK: Real exchanges will NEVER call you asking for passwords. When in doubt, hang up and call the official customer service number yourself.

DON'T BE THIS GUY: The $5 Wrench Attack Victim

While everyone's worried about sophisticated hackers, sometimes the threat is wildly low-tech...

The "$5 wrench attack" gets its name from an old webcomic showing a guy with a wrench saying, "I'll keep hitting you with this until you give me your crypto password."

(Dark humor, but the threat is real.)

A crypto investor in the Netherlands learned this the hard way when masked men broke into his home, tortured him for hours, and forced him to transfer his Bitcoin. They didn't need to hack anything—they just needed him to unlock his phone.

The good news? These attacks are relatively rare and usually target high-profile crypto personalities.

The bad news? If you're posting screenshots of your portfolio gains on Instagram, you might be painting a target on your back.

DON'T BE THIS GUY: The Lost Key Legend

James Howells isn't alone in the "oops, I threw away a fortune" club...

Studies estimate that between 2.3 million and 3.7 million Bitcoin—potentially up to 20% of all Bitcoin ever mined—are lost forever because people misplaced their keys.[2] That's worth more than $350 billion at current prices.

Gone. Poof. Vanished into the digital ether because someone:

- Forgot their password
- Lost their backup phrase
- Had their computer crash
- Died without telling anyone their keys
- Thought Bitcoin was "just a fad" and didn't bother securing it properly

Think of your seed phrase as the master key to a bank vault containing millions of dollars. Would you write that on a Post-it note and stick it to your monitor? Then why are you doing the crypto equivalent?

How to NOT Become a Cautionary Tale

Alright, enough horror stories. Let's talk about how to protect yourself...

(Because the goal here isn't to scare you away from Bitcoin, but to make sure you don't become a Netflix documentary about crypto disasters.)

RULE #1: Shut Your Mouth

We don't care how excited you are about your 10x Bitcoin gains. Keep it to yourself.

Don't post about it on social media. Don't brag to your friends. Don't wear Bitcoin t-shirts to the grocery store. The first rule of Bitcoin Fight Club is you don't talk about Bitcoin Fight Club.

Why? Because loose lips sink ships... and empty crypto wallets.

RULE #2: Hardware Wallets Are Your Best Friend

First, what's a hardware wallet? A hardware wallet is a physical device (can be a USB stick) that stores your Bitcoin completely offline. Think of it as a tiny, unhackable computer that only does one job: keep your Bitcoin safe.

Popular brands include Ledger, Trezor, and ColdCard. They cost around $100-200, which might seem expensive until you remember you're protecting potentially millions of dollars in future Bitcoin value.

Here's how it works: When you want to send Bitcoin, you plug the device into your computer, confirm the transaction on the device's tiny screen, then unplug it. Hackers can't steal what they can't reach.

But remember the physical wallet could be stolen, so keep it safe.

But here's the crucial part: Buy directly from the manufacturer. Not Amazon. Not some random website offering a "discount."

Why? Because scammers have been selling "hardware wallets" on Amazon that came pre-loaded with malware. The bad guys already know your private keys before you even set up the device.

Amazon: Great for toilet paper. Terrible for crypto security.

WARNING BOX: If you buy a hardware wallet and it arrives with the seed phrase already written down, throw it away immediately. Someone's trying to rob you.

RULE #3: Metal Beats Paper Every Time

Remember when we said not to write your seed phrase on paper? Here's why...

Paper burns. Paper gets soggy. Paper disintegrates. Paper gets eaten by the dog. (Yes, this has happened.)

Smart Bitcoin holders stamp their seed phrases into metal plates—usually steel or titanium. These survive house fires, floods, hurricanes, and pretty much everything except a direct nuclear strike.

Companies like Cryptosteel make these backup systems. Yes, they cost money. No, that's not a good reason to skip this step when we're talking about protecting your path to Bitcoin millions.

Also, research the latest crypto wallets with new ways to keep your coins safe.

RULE #4: Don't Put All Your Eggs in One Basket

Geographic separation is your friend.

Keep one copy of your seed phrase backup at home, another in a safe deposit box, maybe a third with a trusted family member. If one location gets compromised, you've got redundancy.

Also if you've got a substantial amount of Bitcoin, it would be wise to separate everything into different cold wallets so that if there is some kind of unforeseen technical error, you don't lose your entire stack of Bitcoin.

The Winklevoss twins (yeah, the Facebook guys who became Bitcoin billionaires) reportedly split their private keys across multiple bank vaults in different countries. That might be overkill for most people, but the principle is rock solid.

RULE #5: The Decoy Wallet Strategy

Here's a sneaky one for the paranoid…

Set up a second Bitcoin wallet (this can be just an app on your phone) with a small amount of Bitcoin—maybe $500 to $1,000 worth. This is your "decoy" wallet.

If someone ever forces you to give up your crypto (hello, $5 wrench attack), you unlock your phone, open the decoy wallet app, and transfer that small amount to their address. They think they got everything and leave you alone.

Your real fortune stays hidden on your hardware wallet, which they never even knew existed.

It's like keeping a $20 bill in your shoe while your real money is hidden elsewhere. Sometimes being clever beats being tough.

When Other People Hold Your Bitcoin (And Why That's Risky)

Now let's talk about what happens when you DON'T control your own keys...

Quick explainer for newbies: When you buy Bitcoin from places like Coinbase, Cash App, or Robinhood, you don't actually "own" the Bitcoin in the same way you own cash in your wallet. The company owns it, and you have an IOU. It's like having money in a bank account vs. having cash in your pocket.

The crypto world has a saying: "Not your keys, not your crypto." Translation: If you don't control the private keys (remember, that's the deed to your digital house), you don't really own the Bitcoin.

This arrangement works fine... until it doesn't.

THE FTX DISASTER: When Trusted Names Go Bad–Really Bad

In November 2022, FTX was the second-largest crypto exchange in the world. Valued at $32 billion. Endorsed by celebrities. Advertised during the Super Bowl. A crypto darling.

Then it went from hero to zero in about 72 hours.

Turns out the founder, Sam Bankman-Fried, had been "borrowing" customer funds to cover massive losses at his trading firm. When people tried to withdraw their money during a crisis, the cupboard was bare.

Millions of people lost billions of dollars. Not because Bitcoin failed, but because they trusted the wrong person to hold their Bitcoin.

(Sam's now serving 25 years in federal prison, in case you're wondering.[3] His customers are still trying to get their money back.)

THE GOOD NEWS ABOUT MODERN EXCHANGES

Look, we're not trying to terrify you into never using exchanges…

Modern major exchanges like Coinbase, Kraken, and Binance have insurance, better security, and actual regulatory oversight. They're not perfect, but they're way more professional than the cowboy operations of Bitcoin's early days.

Plus, exchanges serve a purpose. They're convenient for buying, selling, and starting your Bitcoin journey.

But here's the critical part most people don't understand: **Your crypto on exchanges is NOT insured like bank deposits.** There's no crypto equivalent of FDIC insurance. If the exchange gets hacked, goes bankrupt, or pulls a disappearing act, you might get some money back... or you might get nothing. That "insurance" they mention? It typically only covers a fraction of customer funds and has more loopholes than a tax code.

The golden rule: Keep your spending money on exchanges, keep your savings in your own wallet. Would you keep your life savings in cash in your wallet? Then don't keep your Bitcoin fortune on an exchange..

The Quantum Computing "Threat" (Spoiler: There Could Be Bigger Problems)

Every few months, some breathless headline screams: "QUANTUM COMPUTERS WILL DESTROY BITCOIN!"

Then everyone panics for 48 hours until someone who actually understands quantum computing explains why that's complete nonsense.

Let us save you the panic... and put this "threat" in proper perspective.

What Quantum Computers Actually Threaten (Hint: It's Not Just Bitcoin)

Here's what the fear-mongering headlines don't tell you…

If quantum computers become powerful enough to break Bitcoin's encryption, Bitcoin will be the LEAST of our worries.

The same encryption that protects your Bitcoin also protects:

- Nuclear launch codes and military defense systems
- Every single bank account and credit card transaction in the world
- Government classified information and state secrets
- Your online banking, email, and basically every secure website
- Hospital systems, power grids, and critical infrastructure
- Corporate trade secrets worth trillions of dollars

Bitcoin uses the exact same cryptographic standards (like SHA-256 and elliptic curve cryptography) that protect literally everything important in the digital world.

So here's the reality: If quantum computers break Bitcoin, they'll simultaneously break the entire global financial system, collapse national security, and send us back to the Stone Age digitally.

Losing Bitcoin would be pretty far down on our list of problems if this happens.

Why Bitcoin Is Actually LOW on the Target List

Let's think about this logically...

If you had a quantum computer powerful enough to break modern encryption, would you:

Option A: Attack Bitcoin and maybe steal some digital coins (while immediately alerting the entire world that quantum computing has arrived)

Option B: Quietly crack into the Federal Reserve, every major bank, credit card company, and government database simultaneously to steal trillions of dollars in traditional money

Any rational bad actor would go for Option B. Bitcoin would be like robbing a corner store when you could rob Fort Knox.

The Timeline Reality Check

Bitcoin's security relies on really hard math problems—specifically, something called "elliptic curve cryptography." Think of your private key as being protected by a massive, incredibly complex puzzle that today's computers would need thousands of years to solve.

Quantum computers work differently—instead of trying one guess at a time, they can try millions simultaneously. It's like comparing a bicycle to a Formula 1 race car.

But here's the reality check: Google's latest quantum chip "Willow" has 105 qubits. To threaten Bitcoin, researchers estimate you'd need around 317 million physical qubits to break the encryption within one hour, or 13 million qubits to break it within one day.[4]

That's like worrying your paper airplane will beat a fighter jet. Technically they both fly, but we're talking about completely different leagues here.

The Great Quantum Prediction Reversal

In January 2025, Nvidia CEO Jensen Huang made headlines by claiming that "very useful" quantum computers were probably 20 years away. Quantum computing stocks crashed over 40% in a single day.

But here's the twist: Just two months later, at Nvidia's own "Quantum Day" event, Huang completely walked back his prediction.

"This is the first event in history where a company CEO invites all of the guests to explain why he was wrong," Huang admitted in March 2025.[5]

The reality? Even the experts don't really know when quantum computing will become a threat. Most estimates put it somewhere in the 2030s or 2040s, but that's basically educated guessing.

Think of it like predicting when we'll have flying cars. Eventually, probably. But it's not worth losing sleep over today.

Why Bitcoin Will Adapt (Just Like Everything Else)

Here's the beautiful thing about this "threat"...

Bitcoin isn't some static relic that can't be changed. It's living, breathing open source software that can be upgraded.

Developers have been working on quantum-resistant algorithms for years. When the threat becomes real (not theoretical), Bitcoin will simply upgrade to quantum-proof encryption.

Just like literally every other secure system in the world will have to do.

Banks aren't going to shrug and say, "Oh well, I guess money doesn't exist anymore." Governments aren't going to accept that their nuclear codes are now public. Every secure system on Earth will upgrade to quantum-resistant encryption.

Bitcoin will be part of that mass upgrade, not some special victim.

The National Security Perspective

Here's something the Bitcoin critics conveniently ignore...

The U.S. government now holds Bitcoin as a strategic reserve. Major corporations like MicroStrategy and Tesla have billions invested. BlackRock manages Bitcoin ETFs worth tens of billions.

You think these institutions are going to sit back and let quantum computers destroy their investments?

The same government that protects the dollar will protect Bitcoin if it becomes part of the national financial infrastructure.

Its evolution in action, backed by the most powerful institutions on Earth.

The Bottom Line on Quantum "Risk"

By the time quantum computers are powerful enough to threaten Bitcoin:

- Every secure system on Earth will face the same threat
- Quantum-resistant encryption will already be standard
- Bitcoin will have upgraded along with everything else
- The threat will be neutralized before it becomes real

Worrying about quantum computers destroying Bitcoin is like worrying that cars will make horses obsolete. Yes, it might happen eventually. But by then, we'll have cars, and that'll be a good thing.

The real risk isn't that quantum computers will break Bitcoin. The real risk is missing Bitcoin's climb to $1 million because you were paralyzed by theoretical future problems that smarter people are already solving.

Government Risk: When Politicians Get Cranky

Governments and Bitcoin have a complicated relationship...

On one hand, they love the innovation, the tax revenue, and the fact that their biggest donors are buying Bitcoin ETFs. On the other hand, Bitcoin was literally designed to work without asking permission.

The "Bitcoin Ban" Fantasy

Every so often, someone asks: "What if the government bans Bitcoin?"

Here's the thing: They've tried. China has "banned" Bitcoin at least six times. Each time, Bitcoin just shrugged and kept growing.

Why? Because Bitcoin is global and decentralized. If one country bans it, people just use it somewhere else. It's like trying to ban mathematics—good luck with that.

Plus, too many powerful people own Bitcoin now. You think BlackRock, MicroStrategy, and half of Congress are going to let politicians ban their best-performing investment? Not happening.

The Real Regulatory Risks

Instead of outright bans, the actual regulatory risks are more boring:

- Higher taxes on Bitcoin gains
- Stricter reporting requirements
- Limits on how much you can buy/sell
- Requirements to use only "approved" exchanges

None of these would kill Bitcoin, but they could make it less convenient or profitable.

The good news: Bitcoin ETFs are approved in the United States and Europe. That's a strong signal that regulators see Bitcoin as legitimate, not some criminal enterprise.

Once BlackRock is managing $11.6 trillion and investing in Bitcoin ETFs, it becomes politically difficult to suddenly decide Bitcoin is illegal.

The Volatility Problem (It's a Feature, Not a Bug)

Let's address the elephant in the room…

Bitcoin is volatile as hell.

It's dropped 20% because Elon tweets something cryptic. It can gain 50% because some country announces Bitcoin adoption. It can lose 80% in a bear market and then 10x in the next bull run.

This terrifies traditional investors who are used to their boring 7% annual stock returns and .36 interest in their savings.

But here's what they don't understand: Volatility is the price you pay for the opportunity.

Why Bitcoin Swings Like a Pendulum

Bitcoin is still relatively small compared to traditional markets. When big players buy or sell, it moves the price dramatically.

Plus, Bitcoin operates 24/7. Stock markets close for weekends and holidays. Bitcoin keeps trading.

Which gives Bitcoin a characteristic of being a canary in a coal mine, where if a big sell off happens over the weekend, it tends to be a harbinger for a sell off in the wider markets.

Bitcoin is a way for these investors to get liquid fast in order to buy the dips in the market.

The Upside of Chaos

Yeah, Bitcoin can drop 80% in a bear market. It can also 10x in a bull market.

The people who made life-changing money from Bitcoin weren't the ones trying to time perfect entries and exits. They were the ones who could stomach watching their portfolio swing wildly while keeping their eyes on the long-term prize.

Remember: If you can't handle Bitcoin dropping 50%, you don't deserve Bitcoin gaining 500%.

The Newer Risks on the Horizon

As Bitcoin grows toward our million-dollar target, some additional risks are emerging...

Environmental Pressure

Bitcoin mining (the process that creates new Bitcoin and secures the network) consumes about 173 terawatt-hours of electricity annually—roughly equivalent to the energy consumption of Argentina. About 45% comes from coal, 21% from natural gas.

What this means for you: Environmental groups and some governments are putting pressure on Bitcoin. Some pension funds and ESG (environmental, social and governance) focused investors avoid Bitcoin because of climate concerns. This could slow institutional adoption and affect the price.

The counterargument: Bitcoin miners are particularly incentivized to find the cheapest energy possible. It turns out that renewable energy is some of the cheapest in the market and allows renewable projects to reach profitability faster. PLUS, Bitcoin miners can power up and power down at a moment's notice which is useful to help stabilize power grids when they need it most and help reduce or eliminate the use of peaker plants.

But perception matters in investing and spreading these use cases will help further the investment and cause of Bitcoin.

Network Fork Risk

Sometimes the Bitcoin community disagrees about how to improve the network. When they can't agree, the blockchain can "fork" (split) into two separate cryptocurrencies.

What this means: Bitcoin has experienced over 100 forks throughout its history, creating new cryptocurrencies like Bitcoin Cash and Bitcoin Gold. Future disagreements could split the community again, potentially creating confusion and short-term volatility.

The reality check: None of Bitcoin's 100+ forks have overtaken the original. The network effect is strong, but splits can create temporary uncertainty.

The "Lost Forever" Problem

Here's a sobering thought that actually makes your Bitcoin more valuable...

Some Bitcoin will be lost forever, and there's nothing anyone can do about it.

Satoshi Nakamoto, Bitcoin's mysterious creator, mined about 1 million Bitcoin in the early days. Those coins have never moved. Maybe Satoshi lost the keys. Maybe he's dead. Maybe he's waiting for the right moment to buy a small country.

Nobody knows.

Those coins—worth over $100 billion at today's prices—might be lost forever.

The weird upside: Lost Bitcoin actually makes everyone else's Bitcoin more scarce and valuable. If 20% of all Bitcoin is lost forever, the remaining 80% becomes that much rarer.

Even Satoshi posted "Lost coins only make everyone else's coins worth slightly more. Think of it as a donation to everyone."

So in a roundabout way, all those people who lost their Bitcoin are making your Bitcoin worth more.

Bottom Line: Smart Risk vs. Stupid Risk

Look, we're not going to sugarcoat this…

Bitcoin is risky.

You could lose everything. Technology could fail. Governments could crack down. Quantum computers could eventually break encryption. A solar flare could knock out the entire internet, which ironically even if one node still exists on the Bitcoin blockchain, you can start the chain again.

But here's what separates smart Bitcoin investors from cautionary tales:

They understand that the biggest risk isn't that Bitcoin fails. The biggest risk is that Bitcoin succeeds beyond our wildest dreams... and they're not part of it because they were too scared to take a calculated risk.

The Smart Person's Approach to Bitcoin Risk

1. Only invest what you can afford to lose completely. This isn't just good advice—it's survival advice.
2. Start small and scale up. You don't need to bet the farm on day one. Buy $50 a week and see how it feels.
3. Master the security basics. Hardware wallets, metal backups, geographic separation. This stuff isn't optional.
4. Plan for volatility. Bitcoin will crash. Multiple times. That's not a bug—it's a feature. Don't panic-sell.
5. Think in decades, not days. The daily price movements are noise. The march toward $1 million is the signal.

Why the Risks Are Worth Taking

Every transformative technology comes with risks…

The internet has risks. Email has risks. Online banking has risks. Smartphones have risks.

The people who understood and managed those risks early became wealthy. The people who avoided them entirely missed the biggest wealth creation opportunities of their lifetimes.

Bitcoin is following the exact same pattern.

Yes, you could lose your investment. But if our million-dollar thesis is correct, the potential upside makes the downside risk look tiny.

And here's the thing about risk that most people miss: Not investing is also a risk.

The risk that inflation destroys your savings. The risk that your currency collapses. The risk that you miss the greatest wealth transfer in human history because you were too paralyzed by fear to act.

When Bitcoin Hits $1 Million...

The people celebrating won't be the ones who played it "safe" and kept all their money in savings accounts earning 2%, if lucky, while inflation ran wild.

They'll be the ones who understood the risks, managed them intelligently, and positioned themselves for the opportunity of a lifetime.

Your future millionaire self is counting on you to make the right choice.

This brings us to the final question: When will Bitcoin actually hit that million-dollar target?

In our conclusion, we'll reveal the timeline for Bitcoin's historic climb and why the window for maximum gains might be shorter than you think...

Important Risk Disclosure: All investing involves substantial risk, including the potential loss of principal. Bitcoin is an extremely volatile asset, and you could lose 100% of your investment. Only invest what you can afford to lose completely. Past performance does not guarantee future results. This is educational content only - we are not licensed financial advisors and this is not financial advice. Consult with a qualified financial advisor before making any investment decisions.

"A million-dollar Bitcoin isn't a fantasy—it's a deadline. The only question is whether you RSVP'd."

Dan Hollings

CHAPTER 11

THE MILLION-DOLLAR QUESTION (YOUR LAST CHANCE TO GET THIS RIGHT)

"I'd rather be approximately right than precisely wrong."

— John Maynard Keynes

So here we are...

After ten chapters of evidence, data, horror stories, and cold hard facts about Bitcoin's march toward $1 million...

The only question left is the one that'll determine whether you're buying a Tesla or Mercedes in 2030 or explaining to your kids why you missed the greatest wealth transfer in human history:

Are you in?

Picture This: Two Coffee Shop Conversations in 2030

Scene 1: The Bitcoin Believer

Sarah sits across from her college roommate, casually scrolling through her phone while sipping a $15 latte (inflation, you know). Her friend asks about that "Bitcoin thing" she kept talking about back in 2024.

Sarah smiles. "Remember when I was buying $500 worth every week when Bitcoin was around $100,000? You thought I was nuts and frankly I felt a little crazy myself."

"Yeah, that was crazy how much you put into it!"

""Well... turns out not such a crazy idea in the end. Those weekly purchases over four years? They're worth about $1.04 million now. I was able to use it as collateral to put a massive down payment on the house. Plus we got a major headstart on the kids' college fund. I work because I want to, not because I have to."

Her friend asks "Do you think I should invest in Bitcoin?"

Scene 2: The Cautious One

Jeff nervously fidgets with his credit card statement at the next table. Bitcoin just hit $1.2 million, and it's all over the news. Again.

His buddy asks, "Remember years ago when you were debating constantly about whether or not to put an investment into Bitcoin?"

"I was going to," Jeff sighs. "I had $10,000 in savings. I read that book about Bitcoin hitting a million dollars. But then I thought... 'what if I lose it all?' and just ended up doing nothing."

"Did you do anything with that $10,000?"

Jeff looks down. "Still sitting in the bank, worth maybe $7,000 in today's money. Meanwhile, that $10,000 in Bitcoin would be worth $120,000 now. But savings seemed like the safe thing to do."

Jeff and his friend sit in the uncomfortable silence thinking about what could have been.

The Convergence Is Real (And It's Happening Faster Than You Think)

Look, we're not going to sugarcoat this with promises of overnight riches or some get-rich-quick fairy tale.

But the convergence of forces pushing Bitcoin toward that million-dollar target? That's REAL.

And it's accelerating...

The Corporate Takeover Continues

As we write this, Strategy (formerly MicroStrategy) holds 628,946 Bitcoin worth approximately $76.5 billion.[4] That's more than 2% of all Bitcoin that will ever exist.

Tesla holds 11,509 BTC on its balance sheet.[5]

Coinbase has 6,885 BTC.[6] Over 145 companies now hold Bitcoin as a treasury asset.[7]

But here's the kicker: This is just the beginning.

Every quarter, more Fortune 500 companies are changing the question to their CFO's from… "Should we buy Bitcoin?" to "Why aren't we buying Bitcoin?"

The FOMO at the corporate level is real. And when Apple or Microsoft finally pulls the trigger on a billion-dollar Bitcoin purchase? (Not if, when...)

That's when things get REALLY interesting.

Governments Are Getting In The Game

Remember when Bitcoin was "just for criminals" on the dark web?

On March 6, 2025, President Trump signed an executive order establishing the U.S. Strategic Bitcoin Reserve and U.S. Digital Asset Stockpile.[1] The reserve will be capitalized with Bitcoin already owned by the federal government - estimated at about 200,000 BTC as of March 2025.[2] Senator Cynthia Lummis has introduced a bill proposing to buy 1 million BTC over five years.[3]

When the world's largest economy starts stockpiling Bitcoin like it's gold...

When other countries feel pressured to follow suit so they don't get left behind...

That's not speculation. That's basic geopolitics.

The Energy Revolution Is Bitcoin-Powered

All those environmental critics said Bitcoin would never go green.

They were wrong. Again.

Bitcoin's renewable energy usage has nearly doubled since 2011—from 20% to 41% in 2024, projected to reach 70% by 2030. The Bitcoin Mining Council reports that members representing 43% of the global network use 63% renewable energy.

Bitcoin isn't killing the planet. It's helping to power the clean energy transition by providing economic incentives for renewable energy projects that wouldn't otherwise be profitable.

Funny how innovation works when you actually let it happen instead of banning it.

The Unbanked Are Finding Their Bank

Here's something the traditional finance bros didn't see coming...

1.7 billion people worldwide are unbanked, but most have smartphones. Bitcoin doesn't care if you have a credit score, a permanent address, or government ID.

In places like Kenya's Kibera slum, residents are using Bitcoin for daily purchases and remittances, avoiding theft and a highly uncertain banking industry in their country.

When billions of people who were excluded from the old financial system start using Bitcoin as their primary bank...

When they start saving in Bitcoin instead of their rapidly devaluing local currencies...

That's a massive new source of demand that most Western analysts completely ignore that offers economic hope to those who have lived in financial impoverishment.

Gold's Market Cap Is The Target (And It's Getting Closer)

Bitcoin's current market cap is around $2.36 trillion.[8] Gold's is approximately $22.7 trillion.[9]

For Bitcoin to match gold's market cap, each Bitcoin would need to be worth about $1,142,939.[10]

Our million-dollar target? That's actually conservative.

And here's the thing about market caps: Gold's isn't growing much. Bitcoin's is growing exponentially. Plus Bitcoin presents a better value proposition than gold since it's more divisible and transferable over the internet with no middleman needed.

This Time Really IS Different (And Here's Why)

We know, we know... "This time is different" are the four most dangerous words in investing.

But seriously, this time IS different.

Not because of price charts or technical analysis or some mystical pattern.

Because of institutional infrastructure that didn't exist in previous cycles:

- **Bitcoin ETFs** approved by the SEC and managed by BlackRock
- **Regulatory clarity** instead of constant government threats
- **Corporate adoption** at unprecedented scale
- **Government recognition** as a strategic asset
- **Environmental improvements** that's powering more green energy.

Previous Bitcoin bull runs were driven by retail speculation and hype.

This one is being driven by the largest financial institutions in the world systematically adding and offering Bitcoin in their portfolios.

That's not speculation. That's structural change.

The Historic Parallel You Need to Understand

Want to know what this Bitcoin moment feels like?

It's 1995, and you're watching the early days of the Internet.

Amazon's initial funding came from 22 investors, each contributing $50,000. Bezos' parents invested $245,573 in 1995—an investment that could now be worth as much as $30 billion, a return of approximately 12,000,000%.[11]

If you had invested $1,000 in Amazon stock 20 years ago, it would today be worth about $105,000. That's an annualized total return of 26.2%.[12]

Microsoft's IPO investors who put in $1,000 in 1986 would have $3.23 million today—a return of 327,401%.[13]

Here's the thing that most people miss: The Internet created the greatest wealth transfer in modern history. But it wasn't just the companies that got rich.

It was the early adopters and investors who took a chance. The people who understood the technology before it was obvious.

The people who bought Amazon stock when "selling books online" sounded ridiculous.

The people who bought Microsoft when "computer software" was a niche market.

The people who understood that these weren't just investments—they were bets on the future.

Bitcoin is the same opportunity.

A Future Scenario (or A Path to Bitcoin hitting $1 Million in the next 4 years)

Forget the two-scenario consultant approach. Here's how we actually think this unfolds:

2025: The institutional dominoes start falling. The Strategic Bitcoin Reserve is already established.[14] More S&P 500 companies add Bitcoin to their balance sheets amid constant "new all-time high" headlines.

2026: Other countries scramble to establish their own Bitcoin reserves. FOMO hits maximum intensity as everyday investors watch their neighbors get rich. Bitcoin approaches $300,000.

2027: The supply crunch becomes undeniable. With only 21 million Bitcoin ever to exist, and institutions hoarding, retail availability becomes scarce. Price discovery gets weird. Bitcoin hits $500,000 amid wild volatility.

2028: The halvening hits during maximum institutional demand. Mining rewards cut in half just as global governments and corporations are desperately trying to acquire Bitcoin. Supply shock meets demand shock. We cross $1 million.

Could it happen faster? Absolutely.

Could it take longer? Absolutely.

But we believe that the million dollar Bitcoin is inevitable. It's really just about when you decide to hop in.

The Math That Should Keep You Up at Night

Let's make this real with actual numbers...

Conservative weekly DCA starting today:

- $50 per week for 4 years = $10,400 invested
- If Bitcoin reaches $1 million = approximately $104,000 return
- 10x your money over 4 years

Aggressive weekly DCA:

- $200 per week for 4 years = $41,600 invested
- If Bitcoin reaches $1 million = approximately $416,000 return
- Enough to buy a house in cash

The opportunity cost of waiting:

- That $10,400 sitting in savings at 3% interest = $11,700 in 4 years
- That same money in Bitcoin at $1 million = $104,000
- You just cost yourself $92,300 by playing it "safe"

The One Thing That Separates Wealthy People From Everyone Else

FOMO is a powerful psychological phenomenon that can affect investors of all skill levels. Fear of missing out on potential profits can lead investors to make rash and impulsive decisions.

But here's what wealthy people understand that broke people don't:

The biggest risk isn't losing money on an investment.

The biggest risk is missing the investment entirely.

Fear of loss and financial insecurity can lead to overly conservative investment decisions. Greed and overconfidence can lead to excessive risk-taking.

The magic happens in the middle: calculated risk-taking based on solid research.

We've given you the research. We've shown you the trends. We've laid out the case.

The only question is: Do you have the courage to act on it?

What Smart Money Does While Everyone Else Debates

If you've made it this far in the book, you're already ahead of 99% of people who are still asking "What is Bitcoin?"

Here's what the smart money does while everyone else is still debating whether crypto is "real":

Start immediately. Not next week. Not after you "do more research." Today. Buy $50 worth. See how it feels. Get comfortable with the technology.

Automate everything. Dollar-cost averaging (DCA) reduces the impact of market volatility by investing a smaller amount into an asset on a regular schedule. DCA eliminates the need to time the market. Set up automatic weekly purchases. Don't try to time the market. Just consistently accumulate.

Ignore the contrarians. While DCA is psychologically soothing, some argue that if you have conviction about Bitcoin's long-term trajectory, lump-sum investing might outperform DCA in a rising market. Do what feels right for YOUR risk tolerance. But do something.

Secure your holdings properly. Hardware wallet. Metal backup. Geographic separation. Follow the security guidelines from Chapter 10 like your financial future depends on it (because it does).

Think in decades, not days. The daily price movements are noise. The march toward $1 million is the signal.

Only invest what you can afford to lose completely. This isn't optional advice. This is survival advice.

Your Move

So here's where we are:

You now know WHY Bitcoin is headed to $1 million.

You know WHAT forces are driving it there.

You know HOW to position yourself safely for the opportunity.

You know WHEN it's likely to happen.

The only thing left is the most important question of all:

What are you going to do about it?

We don't know when Bitcoin will go past a million dollars.

This book was written with the intention of getting you off the sidelines so that you can celebrate life-changing wealth and even if you decide not to invest at all…

Either way, you'll remember this moment.

This exact moment when you had all the information you needed to make a choice.

Don't let it be the moment you look back on with regret.

The Choice That Will Define Your Financial Future

We sleep like babies at night because our research points to the most probable outcome: Bitcoin is worth $1 million dollars (and potentially more).

Not because we're reckless gamblers.

Because we've done the work. We've seen institutional adoption. We've watched the governments accept and even champion it. We've studied the supply dynamics.

This isn't speculation anymore. It's math.

But here's what we also know: NOT buying Bitcoin is also a risk.

The risk that inflation destroys your cash savings is basically at 100%.

The risk that your government devalues your currency is basically at 100%.

The risk that you miss the greatest wealth transfer in human history because you were too scared to take a calculated bet on the future.

The tree was planted 15 years ago when Satoshi mined the first block.

But the second best time to plant your tree?

Right now.

Today.

This minute.

And if you're reading this book and Bitcoin is already at $1 Million, please go ahead and pick up our other book… the $2 Million Dollar Bitcoin.

The greatest wealth transfer in human history is happening with or without you.

The only question is which side of it you want to be on.

Will you be joining?

Final Risk Disclosure: Bitcoin is extremely volatile and you could lose 100% of your investment. This is educational content only, not financial advice. Only invest what you can afford to lose completely. Past performance doesn't guarantee future results. Do your own research and consult with qualified financial advisors before making investment decisions. The authors may hold Bitcoin and other cryptocurrencies.

THE MILLION DOLLAR BITCOIN - GLOSSARY OF TERMS

How to Use This Glossary

This glossary contains essential Bitcoin and cryptocurrency terms to help you understand the concepts discussed throughout this book. While every term mentioned in the main text is included here, we've also added important related terms you may encounter in your Bitcoin journey, even if they weren't specifically covered in the chapters above.

Terms are arranged alphabetically for easy reference. If you're reading the book and come across an unfamiliar term, simply flip to this section to find a clear, jargon-free explanation.

Note: Some terms included here extend beyond what's covered in the main book but are commonly encountered in Bitcoin discussions, news, and other educational materials. These additional terms will help you navigate the broader Bitcoin ecosystem with confidence.

51% Attack - A theoretical attack where someone controls more than half the network's mining power, allowing them to manipulate transactions. Extremely expensive and increasingly impractical as Bitcoin grows.

AML/KYC - Anti-Money Laundering/Know Your Customer regulations requiring exchanges to verify user identities.

Adoption Curve - The typical pattern of new technology adoption, from innovators to early adopters to mainstream users.

Arbitrage - Profiting from price differences of Bitcoin across different exchanges or markets.

Bear Market - Extended period of declining Bitcoin prices, often 50-80% drops from peaks.

Bitcoin (BTC) - The world's first cryptocurrency, created by Satoshi Nakamoto in 2009. A decentralized digital currency that operates without a central authority, limited to 21 million coins forever.

Bitcoin Mining - The process of using specialized computers to verify transactions and add new blocks to the blockchain. Miners are rewarded with new Bitcoin.

Bitcoin Rainbow Chart - A logarithmic chart overlaying rainbow-colored bands to indicate whether Bitcoin is undervalued or overvalued at any given time.

Blockchain - The underlying technology of Bitcoin; a distributed ledger that records all Bitcoin transactions across a network of computers in chronological order.

Bull Market - Extended period of rising Bitcoin prices and positive sentiment.

Censorship Resistance - Bitcoin's ability to process transactions regardless of political or economic pressure.

Cold Wallet - Offline Bitcoin storage, typically hardware devices. More secure but less convenient for frequent transactions.

Collateralization - Using Bitcoin as security for loans or other financial products.

Consensus - Agreement among network participants on the validity of transactions and blocks.

Counterparty Risk - Risk that the other party in a transaction won't fulfill their obligations.

Custody Risk - Risk of losing Bitcoin due to theft, loss of keys, or exchange failures.

Cyprus Crisis - 2013 banking crisis that drove Bitcoin adoption as people sought alternatives to traditional banking.

Decentralization - Distribution of control across many participants rather than a single authority.

DePIN - Decentralized Physical Infrastructure Networks using Bitcoin incentives to build real-world infrastructure.

Diamond Hands - Holding Bitcoin through extreme volatility without selling. Opposite of "paper hands" (selling at the first sign of trouble).

Difficulty Adjustment - Bitcoin automatically adjusts mining difficulty every 2,016 blocks (approximately 2 weeks) to maintain 10-minute block times.

Dollar-Cost Averaging (DCA) - Investing a fixed amount regularly regardless of price, helping smooth out volatility over time.

Energy Intensity - The amount of electricity Bitcoin mining consumes, currently about 173 terawatt-hours annually.

ETF (Exchange-Traded Fund) - Investment funds that trade on stock exchanges. Bitcoin ETFs allow traditional investors to gain Bitcoin exposure without directly buying Bitcoin.

Exchange Hacks - Losing Bitcoin stored on centralized exchanges that get hacked.

Fear and Greed Index - A sentiment indicator measuring market emotions from 0 (extreme fear) to 100 (extreme greed).

Fiat Currency - Government-issued currency not backed by physical commodities like gold (USD, EUR, JPY).

Flared Gas - Natural gas burned off as waste during oil extraction. Bitcoin miners can capture this waste energy for mining operations.

FOMO - Fear of Missing Out. The anxiety that Bitcoin will continue rising without you, often leading to impulsive buying.

FOMO Buying - Purchasing Bitcoin during price peaks due to fear of missing out.

Fork - A change to Bitcoin's protocol rules. Can be "soft" (backward compatible) or "hard" (creating a new cryptocurrency).

FUD - Fear, Uncertainty, and Doubt. Often spread to manipulate Bitcoin prices downward.

Futures - Contracts to buy or sell Bitcoin at a predetermined price on a future date.

Genesis Block - The first block of the Bitcoin blockchain, mined by Satoshi Nakamoto on January 3, 2009, containing the message about bank bailouts.

Grid Balancing - Using Bitcoin miners as flexible electrical loads that can instantly shut down to stabilize power grids during emergencies.

Halvening (Halving) - An event that occurs approximately every four years where the reward for mining new Bitcoin is cut in half, reducing new supply.

Hardware Wallet - A physical device (like a USB stick) that stores Bitcoin private keys offline. Popular brands include Ledger, Trezor, and ColdCard.

Hash Rate - The total computational power securing the Bitcoin network. Higher hash rate means more security.

HODL - Originally a typo for "HOLD," now means holding Bitcoin long-term regardless of price volatility. Originated from a 2013 BitcoinTalk forum post.

Hot Wallet - A Bitcoin wallet connected to the internet (like mobile apps or browser extensions). Convenient but more vulnerable to hacking.

Inflation - The decrease in purchasing power of money over time as prices rise.

Institutional Adoption - Large organizations (banks, corporations, governments) adding Bitcoin to their balance sheets or operations.

Legal Tender - Official currency status. El Salvador made Bitcoin legal tender in 2021 but revoked it in 2025.

Leverage - Borrowing money to amplify trading positions, increasing both potential gains and losses.

Lightning Network - A second-layer solution enabling faster, cheaper Bitcoin transactions by opening payment channels between users.

Liquidation - Forced selling of positions when losses exceed available collateral in leveraged trading.

Lost Keys - Permanently losing access to Bitcoin by misplacing private keys or seed phrases.

Market Cap - The total value of all Bitcoin in circulation (price per Bitcoin × total supply). Currently around $2.36 trillion.

Medium of Exchange - Something widely accepted as payment. Bitcoin's growing use case globally.

Metcalfe's Law - The idea that a network's value is proportional to the square of its users, often applied to Bitcoin adoption.

Monetary Policy - Government and central bank actions affecting money supply and interest rates.

Mt. Gox - Early Bitcoin exchange that collapsed in 2014 after losing 850,000 Bitcoin to hackers.

Multi-signature (Multisig) - A security feature requiring multiple private keys to authorize a Bitcoin transaction, like needing multiple keys to open a safe deposit box.

Network Effect - The phenomenon where Bitcoin becomes more valuable as more people use it, creating self-reinforcing growth.

Node - A computer that maintains a copy of the Bitcoin blockchain and helps validate transactions. More nodes = more decentralization.

Not Your Keys, Not Your Cheese - A popular saying meaning if you don't control the private keys, you don't truly own the Bitcoin (someone else does).

Off-ramp - Services that allow conversion from Bitcoin to traditional currencies.

On-ramp - Services that allow conversion from traditional currencies to Bitcoin.

Panic Selling - Selling Bitcoin during crashes due to emotional decision-making.

Paper Hands - Selling Bitcoin too early due to inability to handle volatility.

Paper Wallet - Bitcoin keys printed on paper. Now largely obsolete due to security risks and inconvenience.

Permissionless - No need to ask permission or get approval to use Bitcoin or build on the network.

Pizza Day - May 22, 2010, when Laszlo Hanyecz bought two pizzas for 10,000 Bitcoin, creating the first real-world Bitcoin price.

Private Key - A 64-character string that proves ownership of Bitcoin. Think of it as the digital deed to your Bitcoin. Lose this, lose your Bitcoin forever.

Proof of Work - Bitcoin's consensus mechanism requiring miners to solve computational puzzles to add blocks and secure the network.

Quantum Risk - Theoretical future threat from quantum computers potentially breaking Bitcoin's encryption.

Regulatory Capture - When regulatory agencies advance the interests they're supposed to regulate rather than the public interest.

Regulatory Risk - Risk of government actions negatively affecting Bitcoin's value or usability.

Rekt - Cryptocurrency slang for getting "wrecked" by losing money on bad trades or investments.

Renewable Energy - Clean energy sources like solar, wind, and hydroelectric power increasingly used for Bitcoin mining.

Retail Investor - Individual investors as opposed to large institutions.

Satoshi (sat) - The smallest unit of Bitcoin, named after its creator. 1 Bitcoin = 100 million satoshis.

Satoshi Nakamoto - The pseudonymous creator(s) of Bitcoin who published the Bitcoin whitepaper in 2008 and mined the first Bitcoin block. Identity remains unknown.

Scarcity - Limited supply. Bitcoin's 21 million coin limit creates absolute scarcity unlike fiat currencies.

Seed Phrase - A human-readable backup of your private key, typically 12 or 24 words like "apple bicycle mountain thunder." Can recreate access to your Bitcoin from anywhere.

Segregated Witness (SegWit) - A Bitcoin upgrade that increased transaction capacity and enabled advanced features like the Lightning Network.

Silk Road - Dark web marketplace that used Bitcoin, shut down by FBI in 2013.

Slippage - The difference between expected and actual execution price of a Bitcoin trade.

Social Engineering - Being tricked into revealing private keys or sending Bitcoin to scammers.

Spot Price - The current market price of Bitcoin for immediate delivery.

Stock-to-Flow Model - A valuation model comparing Bitcoin's existing supply (stock) to new production (flow), treating Bitcoin like a scarce commodity.

Store of Value - An asset that maintains its worth over time. Bitcoin is often called "digital gold" for this property.

Strategic Bitcoin Reserve - Government holdings of Bitcoin as a treasury asset, similar to gold reserves.

Support and Resistance - Price levels where Bitcoin tends to stop falling (support) or rising (resistance).

To the Moon - Expression indicating belief that Bitcoin's price will rise dramatically.

Unit of Account - A standard measurement of value. Bitcoin can serve this function but volatility currently limits adoption.

Volatility - Bitcoin's tendency for large price swings in short periods.

Whale - An individual or entity holding large amounts of Bitcoin, capable of influencing market prices.

ENDNOTES

Chapter 1

1. Warren Buffett called Bitcoin "probably rat poison squared" at Berkshire Hathaway's 2018 annual shareholder meeting. See: CNBC, "Warren Buffett says bitcoin is 'probably rat poison squared,'" May 5, 2018, https://www.cnbc.com/2018/05/05/warren-buffett-says-bitcoin-is-probably-rat-poison-squared.html
2. Avant Garde Aspen Luxury Real Estate reports that Carbondale, Colorado home values increased 460% from 2004-2024, from $256,998 to over $1.44 million. See: "Cities Where Home Values Have Grown the Most Over the Last 20 Years - Carbondale, Colorado is 1st in the Nation," https://avantgardeaspen.com/blog/cities-where-home-values-have-grown-the-most-over-the-last-20-years-carbondale-colorado-is-1st-in-the-nation-or-avant-garde-aspen-luxury-real-estate
3. Gold price appreciation calculated from historical gold prices over past 20 years. Gold traded around $400-450 in 2004-2005 and reached over $2,000 in 2024.
4. Monster Energy stock performance data from public financial records showing 200,000%+ returns since 1994 initial public offering.
5. Bitcoin price data from multiple sources: Bankrate reports Bitcoin never broke above $0.40 in 2010 but hit that level in early 2011, and reached over $100,000 in December 2024. See: Bankrate, "Bitcoin's Price History With Charts From 2009 To 2025," https://www.bankrate.com/investing/bitcoin-price-history/
6. Depledge Strategic Wealth Management reports: "The Federal Reserve printed approximately $3.3 trillion in 2020 alone, which, according to City AM, equates to one-fifth of all US dollars in circulation in the same year." See: "The US printed more than $3 trillion in 2020 alone. Here's why it matters today," May 25, 2023, https://www.depledgeswm.com/depledge/the-us-printed-more-than-3-trillion-in-2020-alone-heres-why-it-matters-today/

7. U.S. Government Accountability Office reports: "As of January 31, 2023, the federal government obligated a total of $4.5 trillion and expended $4.2 trillion" for COVID-19 relief. See: GAO, "COVID-19 Relief: Funding and Spending as of Jan. 31, 2023," https://www.gao.gov/products/gao-23-106647
8. Story of Laleh Farzan documented in Bitcoin Magazine: Alex Gladstein, "Finding Financial Freedom In Afghanistan," August 26, 2021, https://bitcoinmagazine.com/culture/bitcoin-financial-freedom-in-afghanistan
9. Larry Fink called Bitcoin an "index of money laundering" in October 2017. See: CNBC, "BlackRock CEO Larry Fink calls bitcoin an 'index of money laundering'," October 13, 2017, https://www.cnbc.com/2017/10/13/blackrock-ceo-larry-fink-calls-bitcoin-an-index-of-money-laundering.html
10. Larry Fink's 2024 comments on Bitcoin as asset protection reported in multiple sources including Yahoo Finance, "BlackRock's Larry Fink calls Bitcoin a new alternative to commodities like gold," November 3, 2024, https://finance.yahoo.com/news/blackrock-larry-fink-called-1-110000148.html
11. BlackRock's IBIT became "the greatest launch in ETF history" reaching $50+ billion in assets in 11 months. See: Bloomberg, "BlackRock's Bitcoin Fund Became 'Greatest Launch in ETF History'," December 30, 2024, https://www.bloomberg.com/news/articles/2024-12-30/blackrock-s-bitcoin-fund-became-greatest-launch-in-etf-history
12. Jamie Dimon's September 2017 comments reported by CNBC: "JPMorgan CEO Jamie Dimon says bitcoin is a 'fraud' that will eventually blow up," September 12, 2017, https://www.cnbc.com/2017/09/12/jpmorgan-ceo-jamie-dimon-raises-flag-on-trading-revenue-sees-20-percent-fall-for-the-third-quarter.html
13. Fortune reports JPMorgan's investment in crypto-linked companies: "Warren Buffett's Berkshire Hathaway takes a sip of the crypto 'rat poison' he once said he would never go near," January 22, 2025, https://fortune.com/2025/01/22/warren-buffett-berkshire-hathaway-changes-stance-on-crypto/

Chapter 2

1. Forbes, "15 years ago, a software developer paid for two pizzas with 10,000 bitcoin. Those pies would be worth $1.1 billion today," May 22, 2025. https://fortune.com/article/pizza-bitcoin-day-story-laszlo-hanyecz-papa-johns-pizzas-value/
2. Wikipedia, "Cypherpunk," August 14, 2025. https://en.wikipedia.org/wiki/Cypherpunk
3. Wikipedia, "Ecash," August 2025. https://en.wikipedia.org/wiki/Ecash and David Chaum's official website. https://chaum.com/ecash/

4. Wikipedia, "Nick Szabo," August 2025. https://en.wikipedia.org/wiki/Nick_Szabo
5. Eric Hughes, "A Cypherpunk's Manifesto," March 9, 1993. https://www.activism.net/cypherpunk/manifesto.html
6. Wikipedia, "Bernstein v. United States," July 10, 2025. https://en.wikipedia.org/wiki/Bernstein_v._United_States
7. CoinMarketCap, Bitcoin price data. https://coinmarketcap.com/currencies/bitcoin/
8. CoinDesk, "What You Didn't Know About Laszlo Hanyecz, the Bitcoin Pizza Day Legend," May 22, 2025. https://www.coindesk.com/tech/2025/05/22/what-you-didnt-know-about-laszlo-hanyecz-the-bitcoin-pizza-day-legend
9. Guinness World Records, "First commercial Bitcoin transaction," March 24, 2022. https://www.guinnessworldrecords.com/world-records/696240-first-commercial-bitcoin-transaction
10. Bitcoin Wiki, "Laszlo Hanyecz." https://en.bitcoin.it/wiki/Laszlo_Hanyecz
11. Telegraph interview, 2018, as cited in BitcoinWiki. https://bitcoinwiki.org/wiki/jercos
12. CoinDesk, "10 Years After Laszlo Hanyecz Bought Pizza With 10K Bitcoin, He Has No Regrets," May 22, 2020. https://www.coindesk.com/markets/2020/05/22/10-years-after-laszlo-hanyecz-bought-pizza-with-10k-bitcoin-he-has-no-regrets
13. Wikipedia, "2012–2013 Cypriot financial crisis," May 31, 2025. https://en.wikipedia.org/wiki/2012–2013_Cypriot_financial_crisis
14. CNN Money, "Bitcoin prices surges as post-Cyprus bailout," March 28, 2013. https://money.cnn.com/2013/03/28/investing/bitcoin-cyprus/index.html
15. CoinMarketCap, Bitcoin technical specifications. https://coinmarketcap.com/currencies/bitcoin/
16. EBC Financial Group, "How Gold's Market Cap Reflects Global Wealth in 2025," June 18, 2025. https://www.ebc.com/forex/how-gold-s-market-cap-reflects-global-wealth-in
17. Based on calculation using current Bitcoin supply of approximately 19.9 million coins and estimated gold market cap of $23 trillion.
18. YCharts, "Bitcoin Market Cap," August 17, 2025. https://ycharts.com/indicators/bitcoin_market_cap
19. Various estimates from blockchain analysis companies, commonly cited in Bitcoin literature.

Chapter 3

1. Bitcoin Wiki. "Genesis block." Accessed August 17, 2025. https://en.bitcoin.it/wiki/Genesis_block The message "The Times 03/Jan/2009 Chancellor on brink of second bailout for banks" was embedded in the coinbase parameter of Bitcoin's Genesis block.
2. Decrypt. "Hal Finney's idea now sees $18 million Bitcoin price prediction." January 13, 2020. https://decrypt.co/16494/hal-finneys-idea-now-sees-18-million-bitcoin-price-prediction Finney made this prediction on January 10, 2009, in a thought experiment about Bitcoin becoming the dominant payment system.
3. U.Today. "Leading Satoshi Candidate's $10 Million Bitcoin Prediction Surfaces After 16 Years." January 10, 2025. https://www.investing.com/news/cryptocurrency-news/leading-satoshi-candidates-10-million-bitcoin-prediction-surfaces-after-16-years-3807570 Finney received the first Bitcoin transaction from Satoshi Nakamoto on January 12, 2009.
4. The Street Crypto. "Satoshi Nakamoto's early partner predicted Bitcoin at $10 million." February 19, 2025. https://www.thestreet.com/crypto/markets/bitcoin-at-22-million-the-math-behind-hal-finneys-legendary-prediction Finney estimated global wealth at $100-300 trillion and divided by Bitcoin's 21 million supply cap.
5. UBS Global Wealth Report 2025. "Global Wealth Report 2025: Wealth growth accelerated in 2024." June 18, 2025. https://www.ubs.com/global/en/media/display-page-ndp/en-20250618-gwr-2025.html The report covers $471 trillion in global wealth across 56 markets.
6. YCharts. "Bitcoin Market Cap - Real-Time & Historical Trends." August 17, 2025. https://ycharts.com/indicators/bitcoin_market_cap Bitcoin's market cap reached $2.350 trillion as of August 17, 2025.
7. Pew Research Center. "For most Americans, real wages have barely budged for decades." April 14, 2024. https://www.pewresearch.org/short-reads/2018/08/07/for-most-us-workers-real-wages-have-barely-budged-for-decades/
8. Statista. "Real and nominal value of the minimum wage U.S. 2024." https://www.statista.com/statistics/1065466/real-nominal-value-minimum-wage-us/ When adjusted for inflation, the 2024 federal minimum wage is over 40% lower than in 1970.
9. Federal Reserve Bank of St. Louis. "The Rise and Fall of M2." May 6, 2025. https://www.stlouisfed.org/on-the-economy/2023/may/the-rise-and-fall-of-m2 M2 money supply increased from $15.45 trillion in February 2020 to $21.70 trillion by April 2022.

10. Ibid. The 26.9% year-over-year growth rate in February 2021 was the highest ever recorded.
11. Coinbase. "Bitcoin Price, BTC Price, Live Charts, and Marketcap." August 17, 2025. https://www.coinbase.com/price/bitcoin Bitcoin reached an all-time high of $124,290.93 on August 14, 2025.
12. YCharts. "Bitcoin Market Cap - Real-Time & Historical Trends." August 17, 2025. https://ycharts.com/indicators/bitcoin_market_cap
13. UBS Global Wealth Report 2025. "Global Wealth Report 2025: Wealth growth accelerated in 2024." June 18, 2025. https://www.ubs.com/global/en/media/display-page-ndp/en-20250618-gwr-2025.html

Chapter 4

1. Security.org, "2025 Cryptocurrency Adoption and Consumer Sentiment Report," January 31, 2025, https://www.security.org/digital-security/cryptocurrency-annual-consumer-report/
2. BitBo, "How Many People Own, Hold & Use Bitcoins? (2025)," September 10, 2024, https://bitbo.io/how-many-users/
3. Wikipedia, "Metcalfe's law," accessed August 17, 2025, https://en.wikipedia.org/wiki/Metcalfe's_law
4. Peter Fisk, "Metcalfe's Law explains how the value of networks grows exponentially," March 18, 2020, https://www.peterfisk.com/2020/02/metcalfes-law-explains-how-the-value-of-networks-grow-exponentially-there-are-5-types-of-network-effects/
5. Wikipedia, "Metcalfe's law," accessed August 17, 2025, https://en.wikipedia.org/wiki/Metcalfe's_law
6. Coin Bureau, "Plan B's Stock-to-Flow Model on Bitcoin: Beginner's Guide," June 24, 2024, https://coinbureau.com/trading/stock-to-flow-bitcoin/
7. CNBC, "JPMorgan CEO Jamie Dimon raises flag on trading revenue, sees 20 percent fall for the third quarter," September 12, 2017, https://www.cnbc.com/2017/09/12/jpmorgan-ceo-jamie-dimon-raises-flag-on-trading-revenue-sees-20-percent-fall-for-the-third-quarter.html
8. TIME, "Why JPMorgan Chase's CEO Accepting Bitcoin Is Significant," May 20, 2025, https://time.com/7287164/jpmorgan-chase-bitcoin-jamie-dimon/
9. CNBC, "Warren Buffett says bitcoin is 'probably rat poison squared,'" May 6, 2018, https://www.cnbc.com/2018/05/05/warren-buffett-says-bitcoin-is-probably-rat-poison-squared.html
10. Fortune, "Warren Buffett's Berkshire Hathaway takes a sip of the crypto 'rat poison' he once said he would never go near," January 22, 2025,

https://fortune.com/2025/01/22/warren-buffett-berkshire-hathaway-changes-stance-on-crypto/

11. Wikipedia, "Flying Machines Which Do Not Fly," accessed August 17, 2025, https://en.wikipedia.org/wiki/Flying_Machines_Which_Do_Not_Fly

Chapter 5

1. BlueCotton official website and company information. https://www.bluecotton.com/
2. BlueCotton Empowers Its Employees with Groundbreaking Bitcoin Initiative, PR Newswire, January 16, 2024. https://www.prnewswire.com/news-releases/bluecotton-empowers-its-employees-with-groundbreaking-bitcoin-initiative-302035740.html
3. BlueCotton apparel maker adds bitcoin to benefits package, Lane Report, March 8, 2024. https://www.lanereport.com/171785/2024/03/bluecotton-apparel-maker-adds-bitcoin-to-benefits-package/
4. BlueCotton's Innovative Bitcoin Employee Program, BlueCotton Blog, June 3, 2025. https://www.bluecotton.com/blog/business/bluecottons-innovative-bitcoin-employee-program/
5. BlueCotton Empowers Its Employees with Groundbreaking Bitcoin Initiative, PR Newswire, January 16, 2024. https://www.prnewswire.com/news-releases/bluecotton-empowers-its-employees-with-groundbreaking-bitcoin-initiative-302035740.html
6. Ibid.
7. BlueCotton's Innovative Bitcoin Employee Program, BlueCotton Blog, June 3, 2025. https://www.bluecotton.com/blog/business/bluecottons-innovative-bitcoin-employee-program/
8. BlueCotton apparel maker adds bitcoin to benefits package, Lane Report, March 8, 2024. https://www.lanereport.com/171785/2024/03/bluecotton-apparel-maker-adds-bitcoin-to-benefits-package/
9. Corporate Bitcoin Holdings Surge 587% Since 2020, The Global Treasurer, September 10, 2024. https://www.theglobaltreasurer.com/2024/09/10/corporate-bitcoin-holdings-surge-587-since-2020/
10. Apple cash on hand for 2024 was $65.171B, MacroTrends. https://www.macrotrends.net/stocks/charts/AAPL/apple/cash-on-hand
11. Falling bond prices are affecting Apple's cash reserves, AppleInsider, October 24, 2022. https://appleinsider.com/articles/22/10/24/falling-bond-prices-are-affecting-apples-cash-reserves

12. Corporate Bitcoin Holdings Surge 587% Since 2020, The Global Treasurer, September 10, 2024. https://www.theglobaltreasurer.com/2024/09/10/corporate-bitcoin-holdings-surge-587-since-2020/
13. Ibid.
14. Ibid.
15. Metaplanet Acquires 1,004 Bitcoin, Raising Total Holdings to 7,800 BTC, Bitcoin Magazine, May 19, 2025. https://bitcoinmagazine.com/news/metaplanet-acquires-1004-bitcoin-raising-total-holdings-to-7800-btc
16. The Rise Of Europe's First Bitcoin Treasury Company, Bitcoin Magazine, May 2, 2025. https://bitcoinmagazine.com/bitcoin-for-corporations/the-rise-of-europes-first-bitcoin-treasury-company
17. Rumble Announces Bitcoin Treasury Strategy, Rumble Press Release, November 25, 2024. https://corp.rumble.com/blog/rumble-announces-bitcoin-treasury-strategy/
18. GameStop Approves Adding Bitcoin To Treasury Reserves, Bitcoin Magazine, March 25, 2025. https://bitcoinmagazine.com/news/gamestop-approves-adding-bitcoin-to-treasury-reserves
19. Michael Saylor's Strategy makes its third-largest Bitcoin purchase ever, Fortune Crypto, August 4, 2025. https://fortune.com/crypto/2025/08/04/michael-saylor-strategy-bitcoin-buy-third-largest/
20. Why Are Companies Sitting on Cash Right Now?, Harvard Business Review, February 5, 2024. https://hbr.org/2024/02/why-are-companies-sitting-on-cash-right-now

Chapter 6

1. "President Donald J. Trump Establishes the Strategic Bitcoin Reserve and U.S. Digital Asset Stockpile," The White House, March 7, 2025. https://www.whitehouse.gov/fact-sheets/2025/03/fact-sheet-president-donald-j-trump-establishes-the-strategic-bitcoin-reserve-and-u-s-digital-asset-stockpile/
2. Brady Dale, "Trump signs order to create strategic bitcoin reserve — and bitcoin plunges," Axios, March 7, 2025. https://www.axios.com/2025/03/07/trump-crypto-reserve-bitcoin
3. "Establishment of the Strategic Bitcoin Reserve and United States Digital Asset Stockpile," The White House, March 18, 2025. https://www.white-house.gov/presidential-actions/2025/03/establishment-of-the-strategic-bit-coin-reserve-and-united-states-digital-asset-stockpile/

4. "Czech National Bank governor to propose $7B Bitcoin reserve plan," Cointelegraph, January 29, 2025. https://cointelegraph.com/news/czech-national-bank-governor-proposes-7b-bitcoin-reserve-plan
5. Christian Lindner, quoted in "Former finance minister urges German central bank to consider Bitcoin as a reserve asset," Crypto News, December 30, 2024. https://crypto.news/former-finance-minister-urges-german-central-bank-to-consider-bitcoin-as-a-reserve-asset/
6. "Brazil Introduces Bill to Establish Strategic Bitcoin Reserve," Bitcoin News, November 26, 2024. https://news.bitcoin.com/brazil-introduces-bill-to-establish-strategic-bitcoin-reserve/
7. "Japanese lawmaker 'Satoshi' questions gov't plans for Bitcoin reserve," Cointelegraph, December 13, 2024. https://cointelegraph.com/news/japan-government-satoshi-bitcoin-reserve
8. "El Salvador Abandons Bitcoin as Legal Tender After Failed Experiment," Tico Times, February 2, 2025. https://ticotimes.net/2025/02/02/el-salvador-abandons-bitcoin-as-legal-tender-after-failed-experiment
9. "New Hampshire Becomes First State to Approve Crypto Reserve Law," CoinDesk, May 6, 2025. https://www.coindesk.com/policy/2025/05/06/new-hampshire-becomes-first-state-to-approve-crypto-reserve-law
10. "Wisconsin pension fund now includes bitcoin," Wisconsin Public Radio, May 16, 2024. https://www.wpr.org/news/wisconsin-pension-fund-bitcoin

Chapter 7

1. HANetf, "Bitcoin in 2024 – a monumental year so far," https://hanetf.com/news-insights/bitcoin-in-2024-a-monumental-year-so-far/
2. Forex.com, "Bitcoin in 2024: The Cryptocurrency Reaches $100k for the First Time," https://www.forex.com/en-us/news-and-analysis/bitcoin-in-2024-the-cryptocurrency-reaches-100k-for-the-first-time/
3. 99Bitcoins, "Bitcoin Price History Chart + Historical Events 2009-2025," https://99bitcoins.com/cryptocurrency/bitcoin/historical-price/
4. BlackRock iShares Bitcoin Trust ETF performance data, Yahoo Finance, https://finance.yahoo.com/quote/IBIT/
5. Bitcoin Magazine, "Spot Bitcoin ETF Approval Was The Most Important Moment In 2024," https://bitcoinmagazine.com/takes/spot-bitcoin-etf-approval-was-the-most-important-moment-in-2024
6. Bloomberg, "BlackRock iShares Bitcoin Trust Smashed ETF Industry Records in 2024," https://www.bloomberg.com/news/articles/2024-12-30/blackrock-s-bitcoin-fund-became-greatest-launch-in-etf-history

7. CryptoNews, "Bitcoin (BTC) Price Prediction 2025 - 2030," https://cryptonews.com/price-predictions/bitcoin-price-prediction/
8. National Mortgage Professional, "Milo Surpasses $65 Million In Crypto Mortgage Lending," https://nationalmortgageprofessional.com/news/milo-surpasses-65-million-crypto-mortgage-lending
9. PRNewswire, "Milo Surpasses $65 Million in Crypto Mortgage Volume," https://www.prnewswire.com/news-releases/milo-surpasses-65-million-in-crypto-mortgage-volume-reinforcing-real-world-utility-for-digital-assets-302386146.html
10. Globe Newswire, "Bitcoin Life Insurance Company Meanwhile Achieves Historic Bitcoin Milestone," https://www.globenewswire.com/news-release/2025/06/05/3094405/0/en/Bitcoin-Life-Insurance-Company-Meanwhile-Achieves-Historic-Bitcoin-Milestone-with-First-Ever-Audited-BTC-Denominated-Financial-Statements.html
11. Bitcoin Magazine, "Bitcoin Life Insurer, Meanwhile, Becomes First Company To Publish Audited Financials Denominated In Bitcoin," https://bitcoinmagazine.com/news/bitcoin-life-insurer-meanwhile-becomes-first-company-to-publish-audited-financials-denominated-in-bitcoin
12. Insurance Innovation Reporter, "Meanwhile Bets on Bitcoin to Reinvent Life Insurance," https://iireporter.com/meanwhile-bets-on-bitcoin-to-reinvent-life-insurance/
13. CoinDesk, "Bitcoin Life Insurance Firm Meanwhile Shares First Audit," https://www.coindesk.com/business/2025/06/05/bitcoin-life-insurance-firm-meanwhile-shares-first-audit
14. Coinbase, "Coinbase One Card," https://www.coinbase.com/creditcard
15. Gemini, "Earn Crypto Rewards with the Gemini Credit Card," https://www.gemini.com/credit-card
16. Decrypt, "The Best Bitcoin and Crypto Credit Cards in 2025," https://decrypt.co/329755/best-bitcoin-crypto-credit-cards-2025

Chapter 8:

1. Wikipedia contributors. "2021 Texas power crisis." Wikipedia, The Free Encyclopedia. https://en.wikipedia.org/wiki/2021_Texas_power_crisis
2. Browne, Ryan. "Texas paid bitcoin miner Riot $31.7 million to shut down during heat wave in August." CNBC, September 6, 2023. https://www.cnbc.com/2023/09/06/texas-paid-bitcoin-miner-riot-31point7-million-to-shut-down-in-august.html

3. Digital Assets Research Institute. "Bitcoin mining saved Texas $18B, boosted grid stability." Cointelegraph, January 21, 2025. https://cointelegraph.com/news/bitcoin-mining-texas-grid-savings-18b
4. Ibid.
5. "These 23-year-old Texans made $4 million last year mining bitcoin off flare gas from oil drilling." CNBC, February 12, 2022. https://www.cnbc.com/2022/02/12/23-year-old-texans-made-4-million-mining-bitcoin-off-flared-natural-gas.html
6. Digital Assets Research Institute. "Bitcoin mining saved Texas $18B, boosted grid stability." Cointelegraph, January 21, 2025.
7. "Report: Flaring wasted $750 million of natural gas in Permian Basin." Houston Chronicle, June 12, 2020. https://www.houstonchronicle.com/business/energy/article/Report-Flaring-wasted-750-million-of-natural-15335793.php
8. "These 23-year-old Texans made $4 million last year mining bitcoin off flare gas from oil drilling." CNBC, February 12, 2022.
9. Lal, Apoorv and Fengqi You. "Bitcoin could support renewable energy development." Cornell Chronicle, October 27, 2023. https://news.cornell.edu/stories/2023/11/bitcoin-could-support-renewable-energy-development
10. "Report: Flaring wasted $750 million of natural gas in Permian Basin." Houston Chronicle, June 12, 2020.
11. "These 23-year-old Texans made $4 million last year mining bitcoin off flare gas from oil drilling." CNBC, February 12, 2022.
12. Greenpeace USA. "Riot Platforms: The Company Behind the Most Energy Intensive Bitcoin Mine in the U.S." November 20, 2024. https://www.greenpeace.org/usa/riot-platforms-the-company-behind-the-most-energy-intensive-bitcoin-mine-in-the-u-s/
13. Browne, Ryan. "Texas paid bitcoin miner Riot $31.7 million to shut down during heat wave in August." CNBC, September 6, 2023.
14. Lal, Apoorv and Fengqi You. "Bitcoin could support renewable energy development." Cornell Chronicle, October 27, 2023.
15. Ibid.
16. Cornell researchers' findings as reported in multiple sources covering the study.
17. "Bitcoin Mining Can Help Fight Methane Emissions." Bitcoin Magazine, December 15, 2023. https://bitcoinmagazine.com/technical/bitcoin-mining-can-help-fight-methane-emissions

18. "Report: Flaring wasted $750 million of natural gas in Permian Basin." Houston Chronicle, June 12, 2020.
19. "These 23-year-old Texans made $4 million last year mining bitcoin off flare gas from oil drilling." CNBC, February 12, 2022.
20. Ibid.
21. Ibid.
22. "These 23-year-old Texans made $4 million last year mining bitcoin off flare gas from oil drilling." CNBC, February 12, 2022.
23. Ibid.
24. "Bitcoin mining using stranded natural gas is the most cost-effective way to reduce emissions." K33 Research, September 5, 2022. https://k33.com/research/archive/articles/bitcoin-mining-using-stranded-natural-gas-is-the-most-cost-effective-way-to
25. Digital Assets Research Institute findings as cited in multiple reports.
26. Various company reports and sustainability statements.
27. Ibid.
28. Ibid.
29. "Texas leaders worry that bitcoin mines threaten power grid." The Texas Tribune, July 10, 2024. https://www.texastribune.org/2024/07/10/texas-bitcoin-mine-noise-power-grid-cryptocurrency/
30. Ibid.
31. Various reports on El Salvador's renewable energy and Bitcoin mining initiatives.

Chapter 9:

1. GameKyuubi's original "I AM HODLING" post, BitcoinTalk.org, December 18, 2013. https://bitcointalk.org/index.php?topic=375643.0
2. Bitcoin price history data from Bankrate.com, "Bitcoin's Price History With Charts From 2009 To 2025," https://www.bankrate.com/investing/bitcoin-price-history/
3. Bitcoin Dollar Cost Averaging analysis from Stopsaving.com, "Crypto DCA Explained: How Dollar Cost Averaging Works," February 14, 2025. https://www.stopsaving.com/crypto-dca-explained-dollar-cost-averaging/
4. Warren Buffett quote on dollar-cost averaging from The Motley Fool, "What Warren Buffett Can Teach Us About Handling Bear Markets," November 26, 2022. https://www.fool.com/investing/2022/11/26/warren-buffett-can-teach-handling-bear-markets/

5. Bitcoin price data from 99Bitcoins, "Bitcoin Price History Chart + Historical Events 2009-2025," https://99bitcoins.com/cryptocurrency/bitcoin/historical-price/

6. Bitcoin Rainbow Chart explanation from BlockchainCenter.net, "Bitcoin Rainbow Chart," March 13, 2024. https://www.blockchaincenter.net/en/bitcoin-rainbow-chart/

7. Bitcoin Rainbow Chart history from CCN.com, "What Is the Bitcoin Rainbow Chart? How To Use It for Market Timing," October 24, 2024. https://www.ccn.com/education/crypto/what-is-bitcoin-rainbow-chart/

8. Bitcoin Rainbow Chart disclaimer from Bitcoin Magazine Pro, "Bitcoin Rainbow Price Chart Indicator." https://www.bitcoinmagazinepro.com/charts/bitcoin-rainbow-chart/

9. Crypto Fear & Greed Index methodology from Alternative.me, "Crypto Fear & Greed Index - Bitcoin Sentiment." https://alternative.me/crypto/fear-and-greed-index/

10. Bitcoin Fear & Greed Index correlation analysis from CCN.com, "Bitcoin (BTC) Price Trends: The Role of the Crypto Fear and Greed Index," March 17, 2025. https://www.ccn.com/analysis/crypto/crypto-fear-greed-bitcoin-price-movement/

11. Day trader failure statistics from Tradeciety, "Why Most Traders Lose Money – 24 Surprising Statistics," February 11, 2025. https://tradeciety.com/24-statistics-why-most-traders-lose-money

12. Brazilian day trader study from Current Market Valuation, "The Data on Day Trading: Separating Myths from Reality." https://www.currentmarketvaluation.com/posts/the-data-on-day-trading.php

13. Taiwanese day trader study referenced in CNBC, "Attention Robinhood power users: Most day traders lose money," November 21, 2020. https://www.cnbc.com/2020/11/20/attention-robinhood-power-users-most-day-traders-lose-money.html

Chapter 10:

1. Federal Bureau of Investigation. "FBI Releases Annual Internet Crime Report." April 24, 2025. https://www.fbi.gov/news/press-releases/fbi-releases-annual-internet-crime-report The FBI's Internet Crime Complaint Center (IC3) reported losses exceeding $16.6 billion in 2024, with cryptocurrency-related fraud accounting for $9.3 billion.

2. Chainalysis. "2024 Crypto Crime Report." December 19, 2024. https://www.chainalysis.com/blog/crypto-hacking-stolen-funds-2025/ Multiple blockchain analysis firms estimate that between 2.3-3.7 million Bitcoin

are permanently lost, representing 11-20% of the current supply. See also: Ledger Academy on Lost Bitcoin: https://www.ledger.com/academy/topics/economics-and-regulation/how-many-bitcoin-are-lost-ledger

3. U.S. Department of Justice. "Samuel Bankman-Fried Sentenced to 25 Years." March 28, 2024. https://www.justice.gov/archives/opa/pr/samuel-bankman-fried-sentenced-25-years-his-orchestration-multiple-fraudulent-schemes FTX collapsed in November 2022, and Sam Bankman-Fried was sentenced to 25 years in prison for fraud and conspiracy charges.
4. Schneier, Bruce. "Breaking 256-bit Elliptic Curve Encryption with a Quantum Computer." February 9, 2022. https://www.schneier.com/blog/archives/2022/02/breaking-245-bit-elliptic-curve-encryption-with-a-quantum-computer.html Research indicates that 317 million physical qubits would be required to break 256-bit elliptic curve encryption within one hour.
5. CNBC. "Nvidia CEO Huang says was wrong about timeline for quantum computing." March 20, 2025. https://www.cnbc.com/2025/03/20/nvidia-ceo-huang-says-was-wrong-about-timeline-for-quantum-computing.html Jensen Huang initially predicted quantum computers were 20 years away in January 2025, then retracted these comments at Nvidia's "Quantum Day" event.

Additional Sources:

- James Howells Bitcoin Landfill Case - Wikipedia: https://en.wikipedia.org/wiki/Bitcoin_buried_in_Newport_landfill
- Chainalysis 2024 Cryptocurrency Theft Report: https://therecord.media/cryptocurrency-platforms-2-billion-stolen-2024-chainalysis
- Post-Quantum Cryptography Overview - Wikipedia: https://en.wikipedia.org/wiki/Post-quantum_cryptography
- Quantum Computing Threats to Bitcoin - River Learn: https://river.com/learn/will-quantum-computing-break-bitcoin/

Chapter 11

1. The White House. "Establishment of the Strategic Bitcoin Reserve and United States Digital Asset Stockpile." Executive Order. March 6, 2025. https://www.whitehouse.gov/presidential-actions/2025/03/establishment-of-the-strategic-bitcoin-reserve-and-united-states-digital-asset-stockpile/
2. Strategic bitcoin reserve (United States). Wikipedia. Updated August 2025. https://en.wikipedia.org/wiki/Strategic_bitcoin_reserve_(United_States)
3. Latham & Watkins LLP. "President Trump Issues Executive Order Establishing a Strategic Bitcoin Reserve." March 25, 2025. https://www.lathamreg.

com/2025/03/president-trump-issues-executive-order-establishing-a-strategic-bitcoin-reserve/

4. Blockchain Reporter. "Michael Saylor's Strategy Buys 155 BTC, Holdings Rise To 628,946 Coins." August 11, 2025. https://bitcoinethereumnews.com/bitcoin/michael-saylors-strategy-buys-155-btc-holdings-rise-to-628946-coins/
5. Bitcoin Treasuries. "Tesla, Inc. Bitcoin Holdings." Accessed August 15, 2025. https://bitcointreasuries.net/public-companies/tesla
6. Decrypt. "The 10 Public Companies With the Biggest Bitcoin Portfolios." April 17, 2025. https://decrypt.co/47061/public-companies-biggest-bitcoin-portfolios
7. Bitbo.io. "Bitcoin Treasuries | 145 Companies Holding (Public/Priv)." Accessed August 15, 2025. https://bitbo.io/treasuries/
8. Visual Capitalist. "Ranked: The 20 Largest Cryptocurrencies by Market Cap." August 2025. https://www.visualcapitalist.com/biggest-crypto-by-market-cap/
9. Infinite Market Cap. "Market Cap Rankings." Accessed August 15, 2025. https://8marketcap.com/
10. 8MarketCap. "Compare the market capitalizations of Bitcoin and Gold." Accessed August 15, 2025. https://8marketcap.com/compare/bitcoin/gold/
11. CNBC. "Jeff Bezos got his parents to invest nearly $250,000 in Amazon in 1995 — they might be worth $30 billion today." August 3, 2018. https://www.cnbc.com/2018/08/02/how-jeff-bezos-got-his-parents-to-invest-in-amazon-turning-them-into.html
12. Kiplinger. "If You'd Put $1,000 Into Amazon Stock 20 Years Ago, Here's What You'd Have Today." April 21, 2025. https://www.kiplinger.com/invested-1000-in-amazon-stock-worth-how-much-now
13. The Motley Fool. "If You Invested $1,000 in Microsoft Stock in 1986, Here's How Much You'd Have Now." December 27, 2022. https://www.fool.com/investing/2022/12/27/if-invested-1000-microsoft-stock-1986-how-much-now/
14. CNN Business. "Trump creates a Strategic Bitcoin Reserve one day ahead of White House crypto summit." March 7, 2025. https://www.cnn.com/2025/03/06/business/strategic-bitcoin-reserve-trump/index.html

ABOUT THE AUTHORS

Anthony Hall

Anthony Hall is a co-founding partner of The Plan who is also Co-Head of the Research and Development team that is always looking to improve strategies and algorithms to help people earn an income using the volatility of Bitcoin and other crypto assets, regardless of what's happening in the market.

He currently lives in Austin, Texas and if not found at a music festival, is probably looking to book his next flight

Dan Hollings

Dan Hollings is the go-to authority on cryptocurrency investing and the mastermind behind The Plan, the world's most popular online crypto education company serving over 16,000 members in 130 countries. Having mastered crypto markets, Dan and his team have developed revolutionary automated trading systems—including the proprietary Midas Method—that help everyday investors potentially build income streams from home while navigating crypto's volatility.

Before Bitcoin was even a household name, Dan was already ahead of the curve in digital innovation. He orchestrated the marketing campaign for The Secret, transforming it from an independent film into a global phenomenon featured on Oprah, Larry King, and even parodied on The

Simpsons. This experience in recognizing and amplifying paradigm-shifting ideas positioned him perfectly to understand Bitcoin's world-changing potential.

Unlike most crypto experts who focus solely on trading and speculation, Dan believes Bitcoin represents the future of money itself. His "wiggle" and "horseshoe" methods have helped thousands of people invest safely in Bitcoin without the stress and risk of day trading, positioning them to potentially benefit from Bitcoin's inevitable march to $1 million per coin.

Dan's down-to-earth delivery and practical approach make complex crypto concepts accessible to everyone, from complete beginners to seasoned investors looking to optimize their Bitcoin strategies for the coming wealth transfer.

Daniel Hall

Daniel Hall is a Wall Street Journal and USA TODAY bestselling author, speaker, consultant, coach, lawyer (JD from Texas Tech University), and nurse (BSN from the University of Texas at El Paso). As Co-Founder of The Plan—the world's most popular online crypto education company with over 16,000 members across 130 countries—Daniel brings a unique multidisciplinary perspective to Bitcoin investing and wealth building.

Daniel is the creator of the 'Real Fast' brand of training programs and host of the popular Daniel Hall YouTube channel and the Money Mentor Minute YouTube channel, where he helps investors, authors, speakers, coaches, consultants, and entrepreneurs effectively grow their businesses and build wealth faster. His background in both healthcare and law gives him a distinctly analytical yet accessible approach to explaining Bitcoin's revolutionary potential and the practical steps everyday investors can take to position themselves for Bitcoin's march to $1 million.

Having witnessed firsthand the financial system's failures during crises like Winter Storm Uri in Texas, Daniel understands why alternative monetary systems like Bitcoin aren't just investment opportunities—they're financial insurance policies for an uncertain future.

STAY UPDATED ON BITCOIN'S JOURNEY

You've read this book. You understand the case for Bitcoin at a million dollars. But understanding isn't enough—execution is everything.

Bitcoin's rise won't be a straight line. There will be regulatory shifts that create entry points. There will be institutional adoption announcements that move the needle. There will be moments of fear that separate the committed from the uncertain. And there will be specific windows of opportunity where the advantage goes to those paying attention.

Reading this book gave you the framework. The Substack keeps you in the game.

The Million Dollar Bitcoin Substack is where we document what's actually happening right now. We track the regulatory developments that remove friction from institutional adoption. We cover the macroeconomic conditions that make Bitcoin increasingly relevant as a hedge. We analyze the milestones that move us closer to inevitable mainstream acceptance. Most importantly, we separate signal from noise—cutting through the chaos of crypto Twitter and financial media to show you what actually matters.

This isn't speculation dressed up as news. It's the real progress points that validate the thesis in this book. When you're trying to decide whether now is the right time to act on your Bitcoin conviction, when you're wondering if you're early or late, when you want to understand what major institutions are really doing—you need reliable information. The kind that comes from people who wrote the book on why Bitcoin reaches a million dollars.

Subscribe to *The Million Dollar Bitcoin* at *themilliondollarbitcoin.substack.com* . Because knowing the argument is half the battle. Staying informed about its execution is how you actually profit from it.

Scan to subscribe FREE…

Made in the USA
Monee, IL
04 November 2026

67383118R00098